Swan Theatre

An adaptation of the two parts of

THE FAIR MAID OF THE WEST

by Thomas Heywood

A programme/text with commentary by Simon Trussler

Swan Theatre Plays published by Methuen London
by arrangement with the Royal Shakespeare Company

methuen

RSC
Swan Theatre

The Swan Theatre is the newest of the Royal Shakespeare Company's five theatres but occupies that part of the original Shakespeare Memorial Theatre which survived the disastrous fire of 1926. The 800-seat Victorian Gothic Shakespeare Memorial Theatre, opened in 1879, had been built with funds raised in a national campaign led by local brewer Charles Edward Flower, who also generously donated the theatre's famous riverside site. In the years that followed its opening, Stratford-upon-Avon, long celebrated as Shakespeare's birthplace, also became a centre of Shakespearean performance.

Sir Frank Benson, who directed over thirty of the theatre's first fifty seasons, expressed his aims in 1905 in terms which remain relevant to today's Royal Shakespeare Company: 'to train a company, every member of which would be an essential part of a homogenous whole, consecrated to the practice of the dramatic arts and especially to the representation of the plays of Shakespeare'.

When, just a year after the granting, in 1925, of its Royal Charter, the theatre was almost completely destroyed by fire, a worldwide campaign was launched to build a new one. Productions moved to a local cinema until the new theatre, designed by Elisabeth Scott, was opened by the Prince of Wales on 23 April, 1932. Over the next thirty years, under the influence of directors such as Robert Atkins, Bridges-Adams, Iden Payne, Komisarjevsky, Sir Barry Jackson and Anthony Quayle, the Shakespeare Memorial Theatre maintained a worldwide reputation.

In 1960, the newly appointed artistic director, Peter Hall, extended the re-named Royal Shakespeare Company's operations to include a London base at the Aldwych Theatre, and widened the Company's repertoire to include modern as well as classical work. Other innovations of the period which have shaped today's Company were the travelling Theatregoround and experimental work which included the Theatre of Cruelty season.

Under Trevor Nunn, who took over as artistic director in 1968, this experimental work in small performance spaces led, in 1974, to the opening of The Other Place, Stratford-upon-Avon. This was a rehearsal space converted into a theatre and in 1977 its London counterpart, The Warehouse, opened with a policy of presenting new British plays. In the same year the RSC played its first season in Newcastle upon Tyne – now an annual event. In 1978, the year in which Terry Hands joined Trevor Nunn as artistic director, the RSC also fulfilled an ambition to tour to towns and villages with little or no access to live professional theatre.

In 1982, the RSC moved its London base to the Barbican Centre in the City of London, opening both the Barbican Theatre, specially built for the RSC by the generosity of the Corporation of the City of London, and The Pit, a small theatre converted like The Warehouse and The Other Place, from a rehearsal room.

Throughout its history, the RSC has augmented its central operations with national and international tours, films, television programmes, commercial transfers and fringe activities. Now, in the Swan Theatre, thanks to an extremely generous gift by an anonymous benefactor, the Company is able to explore the vast, popular output of Shakespeare's contemporaries and the period 1570-1750.

Despite box office figures, which, it is thought, have no equal anywhere in the world, the costs of RSC repertoire activities cannot be recouped from ticket sales alone. We rely on assistance from the Arts Council of Great Britain, amounting to about 40 per cent of our costs in any one year, from work in other media and, increasingly, on revenue from commercial sponsorship. To find out more about the RSC's activities and to make sure of priority booking for productions, why not become a member of the Company's Mailing List? For details of how to apply, please contact: Mailing List, Royal Shakespeare Theatre, Stratford-upon-Avon, Warwickshire CV37 6BB. Telephone: (0789) 205301.

RSC
Swan Theatre

COMPANY IN ALPHABETICAL ORDER		MUSICIANS	
Tony Armatrading	Bashaw Joffer/Second Captain	flute	**Ian Reynolds**
Simon Russell Beale	Fawcett	oboe/keyboard	**John Woolf**
Sean Bean	Spencer	bassoon	**Roger Hellyer**
Jenni George	Queen Tota	violin	**Richard Springate**
Trevor Gordon	Drawer/Sailor/Spanish Prisoner	violoncello	**Alan Carus-Wilson**
Paul Greenwood	Captain Goodlack	guitar	**John Richards**
Togo Igawa	Bashaw Alcade	harp	**Audrey Douglas**
Brian Lawson	First Captain/Alderman/	uileann pipes/trumpet	**Robert White**
	Spanish Captain	percussion	**Nigel Garvey**
Gary Love	Drawer/Sailor/Spanish Prisoner		
Donald McBride	Clem		
Joe Melia	Mayor/King Mullisheg		
Pete Postlethwaite	Roughman		
Imelda Staunton	Bess Bridges	Directed by	**Trevor Nunn**
Philip Sully	Carrol/Singer/Surgeon/	Set designed by	**John Napier**
	Bandit Chief/Merchant	Costumes designed by	**Andreane Neofitou**
		Lighting by	**Wayne Dowdeswell**

The many other parts are played by the company

Music by	**Shaun Davey**
Fights by	**Malcolm Ranson**
Company voice work by	**Cicely Berry** and
	David Carey
Music Director	**John Woolf**
Assistant Director	**Jude Kelly**
Stage Manager	**Rachael Whitteridge**
Deputy Stage Manager	**Graham Watts**
Assistant Stage Manager	**Debra Hardy**

This production is sponsored by

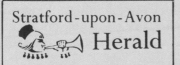

Stratford-upon-Avon Herald

This performance is approximately 3 hours long, including one interval of 20 minutes.

First performance of this RSC production: Swan Theatre, Stratford-upon-Avon, 11 September 1986.

Please do not smoke or use cameras or tape recorders in the auditorium. And please remember that noise such as whispering, coughing, rustling programmes and the bleeping of digital watches can be distracting to performers and also spoils the performance for other members of the audience.

Arts Council Funded

Swan Theatre

Royal Shakespeare Company

Incorporated under Royal Charter as the
Royal Shakespeare Theatre
Patron Her Majesty The Queen
President Lord Wilson
Deputy President Sir Kenneth Cork
Chairman of the Council Geoffrey A Cass
Vice Chairman Dennis L Flower
Joint Artistic Directors Terry Hands Trevor Nunn
Direction Peggy Ashcroft John Barton Peter Brook
Terry Hands Trevor Nunn
Consultant Director Sir Peter Hall

Swan Theatre

Siobhan Bracke *Casting*
Wayne Dowdeswell *Chief Electrician*
Josie Horton *Deputy Wardrobe Mistress*
Geoff Locker *Production Manager*
Andy Matthews *Deputy Chief Electrician*
Philip Medcraft *Master Carpenter*
Janet Morrow *Publicity*
Nicola Russell *Press (0789) 296655*
Mo Weinstock *Sound*

Production Credits for The Fair Maid of the West

Scenery, properties, costumes and wigs made in
RST workshops, Stratford-upon-Avon. Additional
costumes made by Kate Wyatt, Doreen Brown,
Sue Kaye, Jane Heywood. Hats by Elaine Moore.
Production photographs by Michael Le Poer
Trench.

Facilities

In addition to bar and coffee facilities on the
ground floor, there is wine on sale on the first floor
bridge outside Gallery 1. Toilets, including
facilities for disabled people, are situated on the
ground floor only.

RSC Collection

Each year the RSC Collection presents a theatre
exhibition associated with the season's plays. This
year's exhibition, to celebrate the opening of the
new Swan, concentrates on the changing styles of
staging from medieval times to the present day.
Come and see our exhibition; browse in the sales
and refreshments area – and book a backstage tour.

Swan Theatre Repertoire 1986

The Two Noble Kinsmen
by William Shakespeare
and John Fletcher

Every Man In His Humour
by Ben Jonson

The Rover
by Aphra Behn

The Fair Maid of the West
by Thomas Heywood

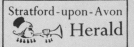

Contents

Director's Note

Just as with many latter-day sequels such as to *Star Wars* or *Raiders*, or *Friday the Thirteenth*, so *The Fair Maid of the West Two* retains all the popular characters but loses much of the urgency and vitality that made the original work successful. It is not inappropriate to refer in this context to popular films. Heywood was essentially a scriptwriter. He wrote or had a hand in the writing of two hundred plays. He would have felt quite at home in Hollywood.

Like the best scriptwriters, Heywood was a barometer, measuring the tastes and vogues of the age. His long career reflects the fashions of successive decades and equally he seems to have been able to predict what the mass of people would pay money to see.

He dramatises the manners and mores of his contemporaries, but not with Jonsonian satirical intent. You wait for Heywood's point of view, his particular poetic personality, and you wait in vain. He sees the world in a mildly philanthropic, mildly liberal, mildly humane and pragmatically journalistic way. He doesn't investigate moral contradictions; he rather recycles the certainties.

So why is Heywood worth our consideration today? Not only because of his whirling narratives and demanding dramaturgy, and not only because he was an entirely accessible, popular entertainer whose achievements provide a fascinating context for his greater but more obscure contemporaries; but because in his adventure stories, he conveys a disarming innocence, an uncomplicated childlike directness which is revealing of the nation's character at the beginning of the English colonial parabola. Indeed it is sometimes difficult to believe his notions of Englishness are of the sixteenth and not the nineteenth century, so familiar is the national self-portraiture. Bess is a heroine, like Indiana Jones is a hero, unambiguous and admirable. The standards of moral firmness and self-denial Heywood requires of his characters are intended to be inspirational and formative and the effect is more of wish fulfilment than propaganda.

In this playing version I have taken the liberty of conflating Heywood's two parts into one, mainly by sacrificing the weakest of the narrative sections concerning the Duke of Florence. This has involved some transposition of both text and incident and a wholesale cutting of lines; in my defence I would argue that all that is best and most original has been retained and that mostly what has been consigned to the cutting-room floor is repetition. What remains I hope is close to Heywood's intention; a comical/tragical adventure entertainment celebrating the birth of a nation.

Trevor Nunn
Stratford, August 1986

A Plan for the Swan

It was in the mid-seventies that an ambitious scheme was first put forward to convert the existing burnt-out shell of the old Shakespeare Memorial Theatre into the new Swan Theatre. It was not until the mid-eighties, however, that this dream of the RSC's Artistic Directorate was to become a reality with the inauguration of the Swan in April 1986 and the opening of The Two Noble Kinsmen. *In an early memorandum outlining a policy for the new theatre Trevor Nunn wrote:*

Since the idea of the Swan was first conceived, it was accompanied by the twin notion of what should be its repertoire. John Napier was first commissioned in 1978 to design an auditorium inside the shell of the Conference Hall: the architectural nature of the new theatre and the parameters of its repertoire were to be indivisible. Michael Reardon, the architect, is now in the process of fulfilling this original brief, and a custom-built theatre, in the most precise sense of the term, is nearing completion – a theatre for the performance of sixteenth, seventeenth and eighteenth-century plays which can be seen as broadly contextual to our house dramatist, William Shakespeare.

Since 1964 we had agreed that in an ideal world we should be doing one play a year by Shakespeare's contemporaries, and we did indeed produce in the main house *The Duchess of Malfi*, *Women Beware Women*, *The Jew of Malta*, *The Revenger's Tragedy* and *Dr Faustus*. However, the worsening overall financial position of the Company decreed that we could no longer afford the comparatively lower box-office response for the annual non-Shakespeare.

Naturally the inauguration of The Other Place provided us with a space for alternatives to Shakespeare, as much as for alternatives to the methods and values of the international cultural centre which the Royal Shakespeare Company had become. So, as a Company, we have almost continuously responded to the imperative of presenting examples of the plays which might have influenced Shakespeare, or the plays which he might have influenced, or the plays which give us, both practitioners and audiences, greater insight into sixteenth and seventeenth-century England.

In the process, we have revealed the existence of several minor masterpieces, we have discovered several exceptions to the 'genres' that scholars might have led us to expect, we have proved that 'neglected' works can still provide tremendous entertainment and theatrical excitement, and we have proved that Shakespeare was surrounded by approaches to dramaturgy which were almost certainly experimental and which can lay claim to being considered more modern and comprehensible to us than his own. And we have only scratched the surface.

There remain countless plays that have continued dormant and which deserve our attention. We have only touched the obvious Marlowe plays, we have never explored the Shakespeare apocrypha, and (bordering on disgrace) we have only ever attempted three plays by Ben Jonson, who in any other language would be the national playwright and have a theatre devoted to him. We have scarcely visited the sixteenth century before Shakespeare, we have never done a masque, and it is high time we tested received ideas about the Restoration, since there would seem to be at least as many exceptions as there are rules.

Of necessity, the key to the whole operation is that the interior design of the theatre amounts to a permanent staging. There is a promontory stage, and back wall that continues the galleried features of the auditorium to provide a sense of upper and inner stage, without amounting to an attempt to 'recreate' the Globe or even the original Swan. It is the simplest possible structure on which we can present the pre-proscenium plays of our dramatic tradition. It is a theatre for texts and actors, for the work of analysis, structure, insight and performance. Clearly, design will have a vital significance in what we do there, but it cannot be design involving changing the configuration of the stage, or even of 'set building' in the sense that we currently understand it.

The task is to prove that these plays live, not that they can be preserved in aspic. And in terms of the first few years at the Swan the task is to communicate and insist on the special identity of the theatre and its policy. So the very first year must not only observe the policy but expound and extol it.

I propose that we should do four plays. One from the Shakespeare apocrypha to establish the link with the main house and the contextual bearing; one early Elizabethan or pre-Shakespearean play to establish the breadth of the territory we are to investigate; one neglected classic from Shakespeare's Elizabethan or Jacobean contemporaries; and one play from the late-seventeenth or early-eighteenth century, to define the opposite bank.

Synopsis

Bess Bridges, a serving girl at a tavern in Plymouth, is in love with Captain Spencer who is about to embark on an expedition to the Azores led by the Earl of Essex. After killing a man in a duel to defend Bess's good name, Spencer is forced to set sail prematurely, but he entrusts her with the keeping of his wealth and of a tavern he owns, called the Windmill at Foy, before departing for the islands.

Once installed at the Windmill, Bess employs Clem as her drawer, and quickly tames the swaggering bully Roughman. Meanwhile Spencer, having arrived in the Azores, is thought to be mortally wounded attempting to part a fray between two fellow captains. He dispatches his friend, Captain Goodlack, back to Foy where, after testing her honesty Goodlack confers Spencer's legacy on Bess. The grief-stricken girl decides to use her inheritance to buy and fit out a ship to sail to the Azores and bring back the body of her lover. Dressed as a man she becomes the leader of a crew including Goodlack, the reformed Roughman and Clem, and duly arrives at Fayal where Spencer supposedly died. There she is given the false report that Spencer's body has been dug up and burned as a heretic.

In fact, the merchant ship on which the recovered Spencer was travelling to England has been captured by a Spanish galleon and Bess and her crew defeat the Spaniards in a sea battle to free the English. When Bess comes face to face with Spencer she thinks he is a ghost and Spencer does not recognise the 'young man' being taken below in a faint. The ships go their separate ways.

Bess becomes the scourge of the Spanish Main until a storm leads to the loss of Goodlack overboard and the shipwreck of Bess, Roughman and Clem. Bess surives only to be captured by bandits, but she is saved by the intervention of the Moroccan Bashaw Joffer who takes her to his master, the King of Fez.

Preserving her chastity against the blandishments of King Mullicheg, Bess eventually contacts Clem and Goodlack who have both survived and they are all re-united on the day Bess sits beside the King in judgment of felons. To her amazement she is also confronted by Spencer. After a tearful reunion Bess begs Mullicheg to approve of her marriage to Spencer. Roughman, believed dead, arrives with the wanted head of the bandit chief and all would seem to point to a happy nuptial conclusion. But both Mullicheg and his rejected Queen, Tota, are casting lustful eyes on the happy couple. Their designs are thwarted by a plot which puts King and Queen into each other's arms instead of those they had schemed to seduce. While Bess and her friends make their escape, Spencer is captured and is only saved by the honourable action of Bashaw Joffer which in turn leads to the return of the escaping English to save Joffer from Mullicheg's vengeance. The King is so impressed with their nobility and constancy that he releases them and loads their home-bound ship with gold.

Commentary

compiled by Simon Trussler

on the full texts of the two original plays

Stage History

The date of the composition and first performance of the first part of *The Fair Maid of the West* has long been a source of scholarly debate. A date as late as 1622 has been proposed by some critics, while others suggest that the accession of a Mulai Sheik as King of Fez in 1604 may have prompted Heywood's choice of name for his own character. But the play would have been even more topical in, say, 1598 or 1599, in the aftermath of Essex's voyage to the Azores, on which Heywood's hero, too, embarks – while the favourable references to Essex, would not have seemed so tactful after 1599, when the Earl fell into disfavour with the old Queen, to whom our dramatist remained unstintingly devoted. However, nothing is known for sure about performances of the first part of *The Fair Maid* until it was published, with the second part, in 1631, and described as 'lately acted before the King and Queen, with approved liking . . .'. This edition included a Prologue only to Part One, and an Epilogue only to Part Two – both later reprinted by Heywood as 'spoken to their two Majesties at Hampton Court' – which suggests that this court performance, at least, was continuous. It presumably took place on one of the three occasions when Queen Henrietta's Men performed at court between October 1630 and February 1631, but it is uncertain whether either or both parts received earlier (or subsequent) public performances at the company's playhouse, the Cockpit.

Not much more is known of subsequent revivals. The early Restoration actor George Jolly is thought to have played Part One in Norwich, so it may have been he who brought *The Fair Maid* to London on 25 March 1662, when two Dutch visitors noted in their diary that they had just seen the play – probably, since the two patent houses would have been closed for Easter, at the old Red Bull theatre, which just managed to survive the Restoration. That the play was evidently still popular is suggested by the publication, also in 1662, of a 'novelisation', which described it as 'so often acted with general applause', but no further records exist of performances until 16 August 1791, when it was advertised, in Stephen Kemble's abbreviated version, as an afterpiece at the Haymarket. Subsequent productions seem to have been limited to those by 'little' specialist societies, such as the Phoenix, which staged the play during its opening season on 11 April 1920, at the Lyric, Hammersmith, or for special occasions, such as the Malvern Festival, where Barry Jackson directed a revival in 1932. Even so, the play has fared better than almost all Heywood's other extant work – with the single exception of *A Woman Killed with Kindness*, generally regarded as his masterpiece, last produced at the National Theatre in 1971.

Thomas Heywood: a Brief Chronology

1574 *c*. Born, in Rothwell or Ashby-cum-Fenby, Lincolnshire, son of Robert Heywood, the rector of those parishes?

1591 Pensioner of Emmanuel College, Cambridge?

1593 Leaves Cambridge without taking his degree, perhaps because of the death of his father.

1594 The epic narrative poem *Oenone and Paris* by 'T.H.' published. Probable earliest date for his first extant play for the Admiral's Men, *The Four Prentices of London* (published 1615), a popular romance in the chronicle form, later burlesqued in Beaumont's *The Knight of the Burning Pestle*.

1596 The papers of Philip Henslowe, manager of the Admiral's Men, record a loan to the company for the purchase of 'Hawodes bocke'.

1598 Contract extant between Heywood and Henslowe, securing Heywood's exclusive acting services for two years. He is mentioned by Francis Meres as among the 'best for comedy'. The two-part chronicle play *Edward IV* first produced around this time (published 1601).

1598-99 Two lost plays for the Admiral's Men, presumably comedies, ascribed to Heywood, *Joan as Good as My Lady* and *War without Blows and Love without Strife*.

1599 Approximate earliest date for *The Fair Maid of the West, Part One* (published 1631), performed by Worcester's Men, with whom Heywood became an actor-sharer around this time, and for whom most of his plays were now written until *c*. 1614.

1600 Publication of his translation of Ovid's *The Art of Love*. Four children of 'Thomas a player' baptised at St Saviour's parish church, Southwark, between 1600 and 1605.

1602 The ribald domestic comedy *How a Man May Choose a Good Wife from a Bad* performed by Worcester's Men – who become Queen Anne's Men following the accession of James I. Heywood married to Ann Butler in June?

1604 The spirited domestic comedy *The Wise Woman of Hogsdon* (published 1638) first played by Queen Anne's Men around this time – possibly the same play as the otherwise lost *How to Learn of a Woman to Woo*, played at court before James I. Possible collaboration with Dekker and Webster on the historical play *Sir Thomas Wyatt* (published 1638) for Queen Anne's Men, who around this time also performed Heywood's two-part chronicle play on the reign of Queen Elizabeth, *If You Know Not Me You Know Nobody* (first part published 1605, second part 1606).

1607 Probable first performance by Queen Anne's Men of the hybrid musical tragedy, *The Rape of Lucrece* (published 1608). Collaboration with George Wilkins on the domestic drama *The Miseries of Enforced Marriage* (published 1607), for the King's Men.

1608 Earliest likely date for his possible collaboration with Webster on the tragedy *Appius and Virginia* (published 1654). Publication of his translations from the Latin histories of Sallust, *The Two Most Worthy and Notable Histories of Catiline and Jugurtha*.

1609 The long historical poem *Troia Britannica* published. By this date Queen Anne's Men had performed Heywood's comedy of piratical adventures *Fortune by Land and Sea* (published 1655), written in collaboration with Rowley.

1610 Probable first performance by Queen Anne's Men of *The Golden Age* (published 1611), based on the classical myths of Jupiter and Saturn.

1611 Earliest probable performances of his episodic 'sequels' to *The Golden Age*, dramatizing stories from classical mythology and legend, *The Silver Age* and *The Brazen Age* (both published 1613), produced under the joint auspices of the Queen's and King's Men (these were possibly revisions of the lost, anonymous play *Hercules*, performed in two parts by the Admiral's Men in 1595).

1612 *The Iron Age*, in two parts, concluding the sequence of dramatized classical legends with the story of the Trojan War, performed by the Queen's (and King's?) Men (published 1632). Heywood's prose polemic *An Apology for Actors* published.

1613 Publication of his long occasional poem *A Marriage Triumph*.

1614 Apparent, unexplained break in his playwriting career from around this time until 1624. Said to have been working on a 'Lives of All the Poets Modern and Foreign', but this was never published.

1618 Possible collaboration with Henry Shirley on the tragedy *The Martyred Soldier* for Queen Anne's Men (published 1638).

1619 Listed among those members of the Queen's Men who were granted livery for the funeral of their patron.

1622 Heywood's name included in the list of the Company of the Revels, formerly the Queen Anne's Men, whose payments towards the upkeep of highways around the Red Bull were in arrears.

1624 Returns to playwriting, for companies under the management of his old colleague Christopher Beeston, until *c*. 1634. The romantic comedy *The Captives* performed by Lady Elizabeth's Men (discovered in manuscript and published in 1885). The biographical prose work *Gunaikeon; or, Nine Books of Various History concerning Women* published.

1625 The tragi-comedy *The English Traveller* performed by Queen Henrietta's Men (published 1633). Earliest likely date for performance by Queen Henrietta's Men of the romantic comedy *A Maidenhead Well Lost* (published 1634). Publication of the occasional poem, *A Funeral Elegy Upon King James*. Accession of Charles I.

1626 Possible author of the anonymous tragi-comedy *Dick of Devonshire*.

1627 *Calisto; or, The Escapes of Jupiter* assembled from episodes of *The Golden Age* and *The Silver Age* (survives in autographed manuscript).

1630 *The Fair Maid of the West, Part Two* probably first performed by Queen Henrietta's Men, and both parts played at court and published together, 1630-31.

1631 Heywood writes the first of his seven Lord Mayor's pageants for the City of London, performed annually (except for 1634 and 1636) until 1639 (the last before the civil wars). Published the prose historical narrative, *England's Elizabeth*.

1632 Contributed to a revised version of Marlowe's *The Jew of Malta?*

1633 Married Jane Span?

1634 *Love's Mistress; or, The Queen's Mask*, a dramatic entertainment based on the classical myth of Cupid and Psyche, performed by Queen Henrietta's Men (published 1636). With Richard Brome, wrote and published the topical play *The Late Lancashire Witches*, beginning a brief association with the King's Men, for whom he probably also wrote with Brome the comedy *The Apprentice's Prize* and the history play *The Life and Death of Sir Martin Skink*, both now lost.

1635 Probable performance of the tragi-comedy *A Challenge for Beauty* by the King's Men (published 1636), the last of Heywood's known plays for the regular stage. Publication of the long didactic poem *The Hierarchy of the Blessed Angels*, and of the prose works *Philocothonist; or, The Drunkard* and *The Wonder of This Age*.

1636 Publication of the prose works *A New Year's Gift*, *The Three Wonders of This Age*, and *A True Discourse of the Two Prophets*.

1637 Publication of Heywood's *Pleasant Dialogues and Dramas*, a miscellany including classical adaptations in verse, elegies, epigrams, and short plays which may have been parts of earlier works now lost (and which probably remained unacted in this abbreviated form). Publication also of the prose works *A Curtain Lecture, as It Is Read by a Country Farmer's Wife to Her Good Man*, *The Phoenix of These Times; or, The Life of Mr. Henry Welby*, and *A True Description of His Majesty's Royal Ship Built . . . at Woolwich*.

1639 Publication of the heroic poem *The Life and Death of Queen Elizabeth*, and of the prose narrative *A True Relation of the Lives and Deaths of the Two Most Famous English Pirates, Purser and Clinton*.

1640 The lost comedy *Love's Masterpiece* entered in the Stationer's Register. Publication of the biographical prose treatise, *The Exemplary Lives and Memorable Acts of Nine of the Most Worthy Women of the World*.

1641 A final explosion of prose works published: *The Black Box of Rome Opened*, *Brightman's Predictions and Prophecies*, *A Dialogue betwixt Mr. Alderman Abell and Richard Kilvert*, *The Life of Merlin*, *Machiavel's Ghost*, *A New Plot Discovered*, *The Rat Trap; or, The Jesuits Taken in Their Own Net*, and *A Revelation of Mr. Brightman's Revelation*. Died, aged about 67, and buried on 16 August at St James's, Clerkenwell.

The Playwright and His Theatre

The career of Thomas Heywood spanned nearly half a century – from the mid fifteen-nineties when Shakespeare, too, was a newly-emergent writer, to the very brink of the closure of the theatres by the puritans in 1642. It offers us a fascinating glimpse of that 'other' Elizabethan theatre which literary critics may with some justice regard as inferior, which social and theatre historians might argue was more truly popular – and which was without doubt intensely productive. Thus, when John Webster concluded his preface to *The White Devil* with a few graceful compliments to his fellow poets, he grouped Heywood along with Dekker and Shakespeare not as great dramatic artists, but for their 'right happy and copious industry'. Judged simply as a workhorse for the theatre, Heywood may have lacked Shakespeare's breeding, but he far excelled him in sheer staying-power.

In that same note to *The White Devil*, Webster also praised the company which had acted his now-acknowledged masterpiece – but roundly dispraised both their 'open and black' playhouse and the 'ignorant asses' who made up its audience. The company was the one with which Thomas Heywood worked at the peak of his maturity and productivity as a dramatist, then known as Queen Anne's Men, and the audience was that of the Red Bull theatre in London's northern theatre district around Finsbury Fields – generally considered to attract less discriminating playgoers than the better-known houses on Bankside and at Blackfriars.

Queen Anne's Men was by that time one of just three of the London theatre companies which could trace its origins back to the fifteen-nineties. The two others – Shakespeare's company, the

King's Men; and Prince Henry's Men, under the management of the astute Philip Henslowe – are today far better remembered, not least for their longstanding rivalry. Both had associations of their own with the northern suburbs – where, as the Lord Chamberlain's Men, Shakespeare's company had been playing at The Theatre before their move to the Globe in 1599, and where, as the Lord Admiral's Men, Henslowe's company occupied the new Fortune Theatre after making a transpontine journey in the opposite direction from the Rose on Bankside in 1600. Heywood's own earliest work, almost all now lost, had been as a hired man with the Admiral's, but around the turn of the new century he found a more congenial role – as one of the 'sharers' or part-owners of the Earl of Worcester's Men, whose existence predated even the act of 1572 which for the first time had given some protection to professional players.

Much of the activity of Worcester's Men until the fifteen-nineties had been in the provinces, but they acquired a London base in 1602 at the playhouse vacated by the Admiral's Men, the Rose, before moving to the Boar's Head Inn in Whitechapel, and then to the Curtain from 1603 to around 1606. By that time they had been granted the patronage of the new King James's wife, Queen Anne, and until 1617 were based at the Red Bull – which, as its name suggests, had been converted from an inn-yard in 1604-5, and was thus descended directly from the kind of premises from which all the permanent open-air theatres took their basic shape. Audiences stood in an uncovered courtyard which surrounded the raised thrust-stage on three sides, or, at a higher admission fee, sat in the tiers of galleries which also formed the perimeter of the building – often hexagonal or circular, but probaby rectangular in the case of theatres such as the Red Bull, built around the 'square court' of the inn.'

All such open-air playhouses were known as 'public' theatres, to distinguish them from the covered, 'private' houses – first used by companies of boy players, but also by adult professionals after 1609, when the King's Men began playing during the winter season at the Blackfriars. Here, there were rows of seats in the pit area of a rectangular auditorium which faced the stage, as well as in the galleries along the sides. Such playhouses were both smaller and more comfortable than the public theatres, and so were generally considered to attract a socially superior class of audience. But a move indoors by Queen Anne's Men in 1617 to the Cockpit – the first of the many London theatres to be built in the streets around Drury Lane – did not revive the declining fortunes of Heywood's company, which lost many of its precious prompt copies in a riot soon after the opening which almost gutted the theatre. After the death of their patron in 1619, some of the players took to the road, while others returned to the Red Bull as the Company of the Revels – Heywood apparently still with them as late as 1622, when his name is among those on a writ issued by the Middlesex Sessions for failure to maintain the highways around the theatre.

For reasons never adequately explained, Heywood does not seem to have written much for the theatre during the decade from 1614 to 1624. By the end of this period, however, a new company was playing at the Cockpit – the Lady Elizabeth's Men, which had been formed in 1611 under the patronage of the king's daughter, in financial association with the ubiquitous Henslowe. By 1622, after a spell of obscurity in the provinces, they came under the management of Christopher Beeston, owner of the Cockpit and an old colleague of Heywood from the heyday of the Queen's Men. The ban on playing in 1625 owing to a severe outbreak of the plague followed close upon the death of King James, and Beeston took this opportunity to reform his company and secure for it the patronage of the new King Charles's wife. As Queen Henrietta's Men, this company then occupied the Cockpit – which, from its original use, was probably arena-shaped, so combining the actor-audience relationship of the public theatres with the comfort and intimacy of the private – until 1636. By that time they had come to be recognized as the chief rivals to the King's Men – not least at court, where Heywood's masque *Love's Mistress* was a great success, receiving three performances within eight days before their majesties in 1634.

Soon after this, plague again closed the theatres for seventeen months, Beeston wound up Queen Henrietta's Men, and Heywood turned from playwriting to a no less prolific output of journalistic and prose writing – though not before a brief association with the King's Men in 1634-35 had forged a further link in the chain by which Heywood had become associated with each of the major London theatre companies of his times. But by this stage of his career, civil war was on the horizon, and the benefits of the old system of royal patronage were becoming less certain: the Caroline theatre was to survive Heywood's death by only a year, succumbing to the puritan prohibition on playing of 1642.

> 'Bess Bridges, the barmaid of Plymouth and Fowey, who goes adventuring in search of her love, is a heroine out of ballad-lore, vigorously and attractively drawn, She leads a sea fight and charms a Moorish king with equal zest, while accumulating money in a practical fashion; she shows almost the spirit of Moll Cutpurse, in her challenge of a coward to fight a duel. In the exasperating second part, this bouncing lass becomes a romantic heroine of the Fletcherian sort, while the honest Spencer is turned into a copy of the jealous Amintor, and the naivety of their adventures among the Moors into a complex double intrigue.'
>
> *M. C. Bradbrook (1955)*

'A Sort of Prose Shakespeare'

It was Charles Lamb who, in describing Heywood as 'a sort of prose Shakespeare', faintly damned him for future generations where he had intended praise. True, Heywood probably shared Shakespeare's roots in the lowlier rural gentry, and also enjoyed with him (as for that matter with Jonson) the distinction of being one of those few playwrights who combined their craft with that of acting, and so derived their skills from experience of audiences rather than from textbooks of rhetoric or university coteries. Whereas Shakespeare so often works by finding the intimately recognisable in the exceptional and the heroic, Heywood, however, seeks the heroic in the ordinary and the everyday. While Jonson delineates a spectrum of society through the satirical microcosm of a fair or a mock-alchemist's den, Heywood ranges through the whole macrocosm – and finds it, after all, quite a recognisable, even familiar place. We stand in awe of Shakespeare's characters from afar, laugh at Jonson's in close-up – and want to shake hands with Heywood's, as our ancestral neighbours.

Heywood's two-dozen or so extant plays form only a fraction of over two hundred in which he claimed to have had a share, yet the stylistic variety of what we do have is both astonishing – and distinctly un-Shakespearian. None of the comedies is quite in Shakespeare's romantic mould, and still less are the tragedies of his high-born, noble kind. 'Chronicles' or history plays there are, early in Heywood's career – *Edward IV* and the Elizabethan sequence, *If You Know Not Me You Know Nobody*, both in two parts – whose frankly episodic quality did little to endear them to earlier critics, but which anticipated his lifelong interest in what we might nowadays call 'epic' structure and accept as conscious choice rather than condemn as structural sloppiness. Thus, Heywood's single 'Roman' play, *The Rape of Lucrece*, goes even further than *Antony and Cleopatra* – probably written in the same year, 1607 – in its concern with the currents of history as much as with personality, while its often-ridiculed use of balladry should find a more open response in an age which has assimilated Brecht.

True, much of Heywood's work was cheerfully old-fashioned – as in the knockabout intrigues of *How a Man May Choose a Good Wife from a Bad* or *The Wise Woman of Hogsdon* – while some were no more than opportunistic exploitations of a topical theme, as in the distastefully scaremongering *The Late Lancashire Witches*. But he could also spot and anticipate a trend which other writers made more their own – already meeting the barely emergent taste for tragi-comic romance in 1602 with *The Royal King and the Loyal Subject*, and sporadically returning to the form in such plays as *A Maidenhead Well Lost* and *A Challenge for Beauty*. Late in his career, he even found himself approved as a writer of courtly masques: but one suspects something just a little tongue-in-cheek about *Love's Mistress*, with its elements of almost pantomimic burlesque, and the rather intriguing running commentary of aesthetic debate which frames the proceedings.

Heywood took the true classics more seriously than such obsequious allegories allowed in the sequence of five plays from *The Golden Age* to *The Iron Age*, which used old Homer himself as linkman for a formally interesting dramatisation of a wide range of Greek myths and legends – which apparently (and probably uniquely) required the combined resources of the King's and Queen's Men for their spectacular staging. He brought such ancient travellers' tales up-to-date in such plays as *The Fair Maid of the West* itself, the early *Four Prentices of London*, and the piratical *Fortune by Land and Sea* – works which fashion, almost, their own distinctive genre of picaresque drama. And there were other, more domesticated dramas of ill-starred love such as *The Fair Maid of the Exchange* and *The English Traveller* (which, despite its title, roams no further afield than Barnet). Always respectful of the middle-class values he exemplified in such plays – and celebrated rather differently in the seven Lord Mayor's pageants he devised, as a sort of mercantile variant on the masque – Heywood gave them a tragic twist in what has previously been his best-regarded play, *A Woman Killed with Kindness*. Here, to transpose the scenario, it's as if a sensible, white, Anglo-Saxon protestant Othello had found his Desdemona truly guilty – and then, instead of murdering her, decided on forgiveness. There's no real qualitative comparison between the two plays, of course – but the moral and dramaturgical issues raised by Heywood's are arguably the more complex and interesting, even if his answers lack quite the commensurate cutting-edge.

Heywood's great defects are, indeed, almost a consequence of his virtues: his many formal experiments were (so far as we are aware) never followed through or consolidated, and too often the narrative drive which impels one through simple or complex actions alike seems simply to be cut short or to peter out once the two-hours traffic of the stage has passed. What remains of most vivid interest is often the incidental local colour – the gambling scene of *The Wise Woman*, the hawking scene in *A Woman Killed with Kindness*, tavern scenes such as those in *A Fortune by Land and Sea* and *The Fair Maid of the West*, and even, in *The Fair Maid of the Exchange*, the atmosphere of a Jacobean shopping-precinct. His world may not often startle or illuminate with its moral force, as does Shakespeare's, or shock us with the laughter of unexpected recognition, as does Jonson's: but (rather like the world of Defoe's novels, a century later) the very ordinariness of its inhabitants can persuade us of their truth, and so garb the often fantastic in the persuasively everyday.

Heywood, the Printers, and the Pirates

There can be few theatre histories which do not pay passing homage to Thomas Heywood by quoting his claim, some eight years before his death in harness, to have 'had either an entire hand or at least a main finger' in 220 plays – the most prolific output even of those lavishly productive days. There seems no reason to dispute this claim, which none of his contemporaries questioned – yet barely two-dozen of these plays survive, of which fewer than twenty appeared in print under Heywood's own name during his lifetime. It's tempting to assume that these must represent the fair-to-middling best of a career of otherwise unredeemed hackwork.

Yet, as Heywood himself said in the preface to *The English Traveller* from which his claim derives, 'It never was any great ambition in me, to be in this kind voluminously read' – and this statement is wholly consistent with Heywood's attitude towards seeing his plays in print, as it emerges from the prefaces, addresses to the reader, and the like attached to the approved texts of his work. As early as 1608, he was asserting, in such a note to *The Rape of Lucrece*, that 'It hath been no custom in me of all other men . . . to commit my plays to the press' – but earlier, pirated texts of his plays had been so 'corrupt and mangled (copied only by the ear) that I have been as unable to know them as ashamed to challenge them'. He berates fellow-writers who 'have used a double sale of their labours, first to the stage, and after to the press', and stresses that in this case he was acting 'by consent' of the play's true owners, Queen Anne's Men – a reminder that such copyright as existed in plays belonged not to their authors but to the company acting them.

Often, the prompt copy was the only full text of a play extant, the actors receiving their 'parts' in that original, literal sense – not just because of the cost of making multiple copies by hand, prohibitive though that would have been, but to limit the possibility of rival companies acquiring the texts of popular plays for their own use. Publication made a play virtually public property: hence, it is often an indication that a play was beginning to *lose* popularity on the stage that it was allowed to appear in print, other than in pirated form. Or, of course, a company might be in such dire financial straits that it was forced to raise extra cash by, in effect, realizing some of its capital – and it's certainly possible that the publication of *The Silver Age* and *The Brazen Age* in 1613, so soon after their first performances, may reflect the economic problems then beginning to afflict Queen Anne's Men.

Historians assume that Heywood's play on the reign of Queen Elizabeth, *If You Know Not Me You Know Nobody*, published shortly after its first performance in 1605, was among the most popular of the period, because it is known to have gone through no less than seven reprints in Heywood's lifetime: yet this was an unauthorised text, which, or so the dramatist claimed in a prologue written for a revival (and separately published in 1637 in his miscellany *Pleasant Dialogues and Dramas*), contained 'scarce one word true'. By that time, however, Heywood's old commitments were long past, and it's notable how many of his earlier plays were brought to the press in the sixteen-thirties – along with the Lord Mayor's pageants he was then regularly writing and which, as one-offs, were traditionally published by the city livery company sponsoring them. Even so, as Heywood wryly points out in his address to the reader prefacing *The Fair Maid of the West*, he was never tempted to bring out his plays 'in numerous sheets and a large volume' – a sideways glance at Ben Jonson's practice of publishing collections of his plays, and pretentiously labelling them *The Works*, a precedent followed posthumously on Shakespeare's behalf with the publication in 1623 of the First Folio of his *Comedies, Histories, and Tragedies*.

The consistency of Heywood's lifelong attitude towards the publication of his plays is all the more remarkable in view of the professional pride he clearly took in preparing his non-dramatic works for the press. As early as *An Apology for Actors* (1612), he took the trouble to add a note contrasting the care taken by its printers – who had accorded 'the author all the rights of the press' – with the 'negligence' of the printer of his earlier epic poem *Troia Britannica*, with its 'misquotations, mistaking of syllables, misplacing half lines' and 'coinage of never-heard-of words'. Towards the end of his life Heywood turned increasingly towards prose writing as the stage became a less dependable source of income. The change was approved by an anonymous epigrammatist of 1640, who entreated Heywood,

> *Fly that way still, it will become thy age,*
> *And better please than grovelling on the stage.*

Nowhere – least of all in the proud defence of the profession in *An Apology for Acting* – is there any suggestion that Heywood himself felt that he had spent the best part of his career 'grovelling'. Simply, to adapt his own contention, it was never his ambition to be 'voluminously read' as a playwright, but to be voluminously *seen*. In that he demonstrably succeeded, albeit condemning posterity to an extremely limited view of his vast dramatic output.

'There is a peculiar oafish simplicity about him which made him unable ever to create a single piece, except perhaps *Edward IV*, which is not deformed by pages of drivel.'

F. L. Lucas (1927)

'The Rich Spaniard and the Barbarous Turk'

Thomas Heywood had a thoroughly Elizabethan attitude towards travel: he was fascinated by it, but there is no evidence of his ever having done any – apart from making the journey from Lincoln and Cambridge to London, a distance considerably greater than the vast majority of his contemporaries would have covered in their lifetimes. Most shared the contempt of the 'character writers', for whom 'The Traveller' always made a good subject, with his borrowed manners, tall stories, and downright unpatriotic fancy for foreign parts. Of course, if one travelled to foreign parts with the worthier intention of conquering or pillaging them, or otherwise upholding the protestant cause, that was different: and thus did the likes of Drake and Essex and Walter Raleigh become the folk-heroes of the Elizabethen age.

Although we cannot accurately date either the writing or the performance of the first part of *The Fair Maid of the West*, we do know about the great 'patriotic' adventure in whose shadow the action takes place – the raid on the Azores by the Earl of Essex in 1597. The gathering of seafarers in Plymouth at the beginning of the play is thus in preparation for what became known as the Islands' Voyage. This was part of the continuing conflict between England and Spain in which – following the defeat of the Armada in 1588, and Philip of Spain's need to divert dwindling resources to support the Catholic cause in France – the upstart English by now had decidedly the upper hand. To disrupt preparations for a second Armada, and incidentally to divert attention from poor harvests and rising prices at home, Elizabeth grudgingly agreed in 1596 to plans put forward by Admiral Lord Howard and the Earl of Essex for a pre-emptive strike against Cadiz, which proved almost too successful: a rush for booty in the surrendered city allowed a rich merchant fleet to flee the harbour, and burn itself out rather than fall into English hands. In the following year a new expedition was therefore planned, under Essex and Raleigh, with a similar double purpose, military and economic – to destroy the Spanish fleet in the port of Ferrol, and then to waylay and plunder the Spanish treasure ships in the Azores, on their return laden with the wealth of the Indies.

The English fleet duly set sail from Plymouth in July 1597, only to be dispersed by a storm, and forced back into harbour to refit. The mission continued to be dogged by misfortune: its military objective was abandoned, and its leaders were so busy quarrelling over Raleigh's 'unauthorised' attack and seizure of the town of Fayal in the Azores that they missed the merchant target. The fleet struggled homewards, again scattered by storms – only to find that the Spanish fleet, setting sail from Ferrol, had itself been dispersed, and thwarted in its intended attack upon Falmouth. English seafaring luck, it seemed, held good even when English judgement failed, and so the voyage entered the popular mythology of the times.

This, then, is the voyage on which Spencer and his company set out, but from which only Goodlack directly returns – and it is to Fayal that Bess follows her Spencer in the *Negro*, only to embark on a little privateering on her own account before putting into 'Mamorah in Barbary', or present-day Morocco, for water and, as it turns out, a spate of adventures besides. How, on the voyage home half-way through Part Two, the company is diverted by a single encounter with pirates to the northern Italian coast is left unexplained by the zestfully synoptic Chorus who wafts them there. No doubt Heywood's sense of geography was as impressionistic as his presentation of foreigners themselves. Thus, Moors, despite their blackness, might properly be invested with a degree of sympathy, and a sort of brooding, savage nobility, not least because their ambitions had been useful in keeping Philip preoccupied to the south, without threatening English interests. Heywood also presents his Florentines in a fair-to-middling light, altogether brighter than the murk in which the writers of Jacobean tragedy were wont to cloak the supposedly Machiavellian intrigues of Italianate lechers and villains. But not even the best intentions of Philip of Spain to launch yet another Armada against the Ottoman Empire could save the 'barbarous Turk' from being coupled with the 'rich Spaniard' by the Chorus of Part One as the joint targets for Bess's privateering ('The French and Dutch she spares', he piously notes). If Elizabeth herself, whose glorious life Heywood celebrated next to idolatory in plays and books alike, could not in person set sail against the Spaniard, perhaps brave Bess Bridges was the nearest dramatic equivalent to an Essex in petticoats.

'He himself lived and died as a respectable householder of Clerkenwell without ever seeing the inside of a jail or the cabin of a seagoing ship. . . . But Heywood, though he complied with the taste of London, was not a Londoner in Dekker's sense, and in his plays he ranged widely. . . . These heroic exploits, whether real or invented, involve familiar types of character: they are the equivalent of the modern adventures in space-ships and time-machines, which depend on contrast between the everyday hero and occasions fantastic or remote. Heywood usually multiplies the heroes, to give the effect of the modern child's Famous Five or Terrible Twins. Three, four, or more brothers or friends act in concert, and are opposed by three or four villains.'

M. C. Bradbrook (1955)

Old Conventions, New Morality

An actor as well as a dramatist, Thomas Heywood was thoroughly saturated in the conventions and techniques of the late-Elizabethan theatre, and continued to write for companies whose respect for old-fashioned plays remained more constant, than, say, Shakespeare's. He still felt sufficiently in tune with Marlowe to contribute revisions to *The Jew of Malta* for a revival in 1632, with his longstanding friend Richard Perkins in the title role. In the various prologues, epilogues, and addresses which garnish his printed texts, Heywood is (unlike Jonson) almost never·to be found in adversely critical mood about fellow-playwrights, past or present – and even when boasting in the prologue to *The English Traveller* that he has used no dumb-shows, combats, songs, or dances 'to bombast out our play', he adds cautiously, 'yet all these good and still in frequent use'. Not least, of course, in other plays of his own. He was, for example, still using dumb-shows in the manner Shakespeare in *Hamlet* evidently regarded as evidence of primitive craftsmanship – for a mimed synopsis of the ensuing action, rather than as a 'show' in dramatic shorthand – as late as *A Maidenhead Well Lost*, around 1625, with no less confidence than in the early *Four Prentices*, or *If You Know Not Me*.

As its mildly titillating title hints, *A Maidenhead Well Lost* employed another favoured convention of the age, and one which Shakespeare himself had not scorned – the so-called bed-trick, by which a lady is substituted in a would-be lover's bed under cover of darkness, either to avoid a threatened rape, as in *Measure for Measure*, or to secure a desired match, as in *All's Well That Ends Well*. Shakespeare's use of this device is, of course, one reason why the critics have decided that these are 'problem' plays which *don't* end well at all – while the less scholarly find themselves musing on the limited modes of communication in Elizabethan love-making (although Diaphanta in *The Changeling* manages to sustain the deceptive dalliance so long that the chimney has to be set on fire to smoke her out). Heywood, of course, treats us to another bed-trick in the second part of *The Fair Maid of the West*, when Moorish husband and wife are deceived into believing themselves illicit lover and mistress. A generation prepared to accept for years that Hollywood males made love in their underpants with one foot on the floor should not, perhaps, complain too loudly.

Heywood's stage directions require what he calls an 'act long' or 'hautboys long' before the Moroccan scenes of the first part – that is, a longer pause than usual, presumably to set the stage with exotic properties. His audiences loved such showmanship, which probably reached its peak in the five *Ages* plays: these required elaborate scenic effects, including pyrotechnics, and some demanding trick-work, such as shooting an arrow across a river into a centaur's eye. Always, scenes set in foreign parts required lavish costuming, in which the Elizabethan theatre made up in extravagance for its generally skimpy settings. The costume for the ill-fated Ann Frankford in *A Woman Killed with Kindness* actually cost £6 13s 0d – thirteen shillings more than Heywood was paid for writing the play.

Heywood's characters, on the other hand, do not always fit into the expected patterns. Even the apparent 'braggart soldier' type in *The Fair Maid*, Roughman, ceases to be a braggart before he becomes, perversely, a sailor. And as for poor Clem, he is a splendid mixture of the classical cunning servant, the clown-fool of medieval ancestry, and the Elizabethan honest apprentice. Heywood's women characters are arguably his least conventional of all – though their role in his plays is pervasive and often central, as a mere glance at the roll-call of titles suggests, and some of his prose writings are, for their times, strongly feminist both in theme and tone. Victorian editors tended to disapprove – A. W. Verity discovering in Heywood's 'portraits of women, a weak and vacillating picture'. But Muriel Bradbrook found, rather, a proper complexity, or, as she called it, 'emotional colour'. In *A Woman Killed with Kindness*, 'the conventional pattern of domestic tragedy is reversed, to produce a most unconventional study of marriage not as a state but as a relationship'. Bess Bridges, our Fair Maid, also bucks the expected typology: she is neither blushing, immaculate virgin nor yet patiently Griselda-like in adversity – and certainly not the easy-living whore for which her customers at first mistake her. Like the heroine of *Fortune by Land and Sea*, she's an imaginative Amazonian adventuress who is nonetheless aware of her own sexuality – and, like the shopkeeping *Fair Maid of the Exchange*, part of her attraction is also that she can turn an honest penny into an honest pound by her own hard work, despite the convenient dowries that are eventually showered upon her. In this, as in the new-look morality of a play like *A Woman Killed with Kindness*, Heywood comes closer than Shakespeare ever did to dramatizing the emerging mercantile values of his age, for the citizen-audiences who were shaping them.

'In the delineation of Bess Bridges, our poet has pictured most successfully a type dear to him, the attractive, wholesome English girl of the middle class. Bess Bridges is the vital centre of the breezy, spirited action, but not a little of the charm of the appeal of the play lies in its lavish colour of middle-class life and the pervading spirit of patriotism. This atmosphere is typical of Heywood. It is the distinguishing feature of the greater number of the Heywood plays, the indisputable characteristic of the poet's peculiar bent.'

Otelia Crowell (1928)

A Bourgeois Odyssey?

The two parts of Shakespeare's *Henry IV*, as of Heywood's own chronicles of the reigns of Edward IV and Elizabeth, were performed within a year or so of each other: but anything from twenty to (more probably) thirty years separated the first part of *The Fair Maid of the West* from the second. During this period – or so the received critical wisdom has it – Heywood had himself moved with the times, and the bluff exponent of Elizabethan popular comedy was now experimenting with his own variety of Fletcherian tragicomedy – a form to which, it is said, as a good Elizabethan at heart he was not temperamentally suited. According to this view, the rough but fluently colloquial style of Part One jogs us briskly along to a happy end for its hearty crew, while the 'sequel' crawls with tortured rhetoric and brooding emotions towards an arbitrarily delayed resolution of intrigues of love and honour, in which characters become mere vehicles for plot or ideas.

Such a view usually springs from a more general belief in the decline of the drama from a healthy, popular Elizabethan form, with a homogeneous audience of groundlings and gallants, into a broken-backed Caroline creature trying to placate rowdy Red Bull audiences with spectacular extravaganzas while also needing to satisfy the effete patrons of the Blackfriars with highly-strung romances of rarefied sensibility. But to concede genuine differences of taste and audience is not necessarily to accept that the consequent dramaturgical changes need also have been regressive. Least of all art forms does theatre 'evolve', backwards *or* forwards, in quite so convenient a fashion.

Part One of *The Fair Maid of the West* carries, indeed, a different narrative emphasis from Part Two. In the tradition of popular adventures in ballad or chapbook, from which its characters are drawn, the sheer sequential excitement of 'and then . . . and then . . . and then' carries the action along until the time for the play is done. But the first part is also busy with the unobtrusive business of establishing characters and contexts, which Part Two can take time to explore and to counterpoint in more leisurely fashion – aptly drawing on the more contemplative 'why?' as well as the active 'how?' of the events portrayed. No one complains when a symphony moves from *allegro con spirito* to *adagio*, and once one accepts that expanding the play into two parts *affirms* rather than breaks its 'narrative' structure – by contrast with the 'dramatic' structure of most of Shakespeare's plays, it never *was* a 'unified', self-contained whole – then problems of dissonance of tone or style at once diminish.

This is not, of course, to make any exaggerated claim for *The Fair Maid of the West* as a 'neglected masterpiece' – but to suggest that we should judge it in the light of its own *form*, a form which *is* theatrically neglected. If Shakespeare could overshadow such a towering genius as Jonson, no wonder such honest, craftsmanlike virtues as Heywood's have been almost blotted out: and more fashionable Jacobeans such as Webster and Middleton better suit the *angst* of our own age than Heywood's gentle optimism – which expresses a common man's view of late-renaissance hopes and virtues. Ironically, the one play of Heywood's which *is* sometimes claimed as a masterpiece, *A Woman Killed with Kindness* is flawed *as a tragedy* because its hero, Frankford, is so much more a man of his age than the heroes of Shakespeare's tragedies. Hamlet, Macbeth, even Lear cannot reconcile feudal instincts with the ethics of a new age: that is part of their tragedy. Frankford *acts* according to such values: that is part of his.

But *The Fair Maid of the West* is not a tragedy. Nor yet, however, is it a comedy, give or take a happy ending or two, in any Shakespearian or Jonsonian sense. But Heywood sets out his own, refreshingly undidactic aims for comedy in his *Apology for Actors*, where the moral ends of deriding fools and (interestingly) of mocking 'foolish inamorates'

are mingled with sportful accidents, to recreate such as of themselves are wholly devoted to melancholy, which corrupts the blood: or to refresh such weary spirits as are tried with labour, or study, to moderate the cares and heaviness of the mind, that they may return to their trades and faculties with more zeal and earnestness, after some small soft and pleasant retirement.

In that sense, *The Fair Maid* shares the simple aim of tales which have been told to offer 'small soft and pleasant retirement' in every generation. It is a sort of bourgeois *Odyssey*, and in the decades between writing its two parts Heywood had not only put old Homer himself on the stage, but recognised – as astute artist rather than moralist – that times and tastes had changed, so that he might now appropriately stress different aspects of action and of characters.

Bess Bridges is therefore *both* the active Elizabethan instigator of Part One *and* the heroine cast adrift and buffeted by events in Part Two – *both* a socially-mobile tavern-keeper, *and* a lost innocent abroad, with only her honour to cling to. And Heywood's techniques are, in short, those of honest, old-fashioned storytelling, in which, essentially, events shape people rather than the reverse, and the tempo changes according to 'narrative' rather than 'dramatic' needs. Our own age, which purports to dislike pigeonholing plays into rigid genres, should of all ages be prepared to allow Heywood his right to choose this distinctive form – no less Aristotelian than tragedy, if we bear in mind that for Aristotle the 'epic' was also a medium of performance, though in Heywood's hands it becomes, well, more homely than Homer.

For Further Reading

In the absence of a satisfactory modern edition of Thomas Heywood's plays, the fullest remains that in six volumes edited by R. H. Shepherd in 1874 (reprinted, New York: Russell, 1964), while the selection of five plays in the old Mermaid edition, ed. A. W. Verity (London, 1888), is still reasonably accessible. There is, however, a modern critical edition of both parts of *The Fair Maid of the West* by Robert K. Turner in the Regents Renaissance Drama Series (London: Arnold, 1968), and of *A Woman Killed with Kindness*, ed. R. W. van Fossen in the Revels Plays Series (London: Methuen, 1961), and ed. Brian W. M. Scobie, in the New Mermaids Series (London: Black, 1985). There are critical editions of some of the lesser-known plays in the Renaissance Plays Series (New York: Garland, 1979-80), including *The Fair Maid of the Exchange, The Four Prentices of London, The Iron Age*, and *The Late Lancashire Witches*.

Of modern full-length studies of Heywood's work, one of the earliest, Otelia Crowell's *Thomas Heywood: a Study in the Elizabethan Drama of Everyday Life* (New Haven: Yale University Press, 1928) remains fresh in some of its perceptions, while one of the more recent, *Thomas Heywood* by F. S. Boas (London: Williams and Norgate, 1950), is little more than a collection of synopses. In between, Arthur M. Clark had written what remains the best reconstruction of Heywood's elliptic life, *Thomas Heywood: Playwright and Miscellanist* (Oxford: Blackwell, 1931; reprinted, New York: Russell, 1967). Mowbray Velte's *The Bourgeois Elements in the Drama of Thomas Heywood* (Mysore, India, 1924; reprinted, New York: Haskell House, 1966) and M. L. Johnson's *Images of Women in the Works of Thomas Heywood* (1975) are self-describing studies of specific aspects of his output, while Louis B. Wright's *Middle-Class Culture in Elizabethan England* has much that is helpful about our author. T. S. Eliot's influential put-down, 'Thomas Heywood', was first collected in his *Elizabethan Essays* (London: Faber, 1934), and among other shorter pieces of special interest are F. L. Townsend's 'The Artistry of Thomas Heywood's Double Plots', in *Philological Quarterly*, XXV (1946); Allan Holladay's 'Thomas Heywood and the Puritans', in *Journal of English and Germanic Philology*, XLIX (1950); and Michel Grivelet's 'The Simplicity of Thomas Heywood', in *Shakespeare Survey*, XIV (1961). There is little that has dealt specifically with Heywood's place in the theatre, as distinct from the drama, but Andrew Gurr's *The Shakespearean Stage* (Cambridge University Press, second ed., 1980) and *The Revels History of Drama in English, Volume IV: 1613-1660* (London: Methuen, 1981) both provide useful context, while the work of Gerald Eades Bentley is more than usually valuable as background, notably his *The Profession of Dramatist in Shakespeare's Time* (Princeton University Press, 1971). Other relevant studies from which quotations are included here are M. C. Bradbrook's *The Growth and Structure of Elizabethan Comedy* (London: Chatto and Windus, 1955) and L. C. Knights's *Drama and Society in the Age of Jonson* (London: Chatto and Windus, 1937).

'Heywood is a sort of *prose* Shakespeare. His scenes are to the full as natural and affecting. But we miss the *poet*, that which in Shakespeare always appears out and above the surface of *the nature*.'

Charles Lamb (1808)

'If I were to be consulted as to a reprint of our old English dramatists, I should advise to begin with the collected plays of Heywood. He was a fellow actor, and fellow dramatist, with Shakespeare. He possessed not the imagination of the latter; but in all those qualities which gained for Shakespeare the attribute of *gentle*, he was not inferior to him. Generosity, courtesy, temperance in the depths of passion; sweetness, in a word, and gentleness; Christianism; and true hearty Anglicism of feelings, shaping that Christianism; shine throughout his beautiful writings in a manner more conspicuous than in those of Shakespeare, but only more conspicuous, inasmuch as in Heywood these qualities are primary, in the other subordinate to poetry. . . . His plots are almost invariably English. I am sometimes jealous that Shakespeare laid so few of his scenes at home.'

Charles Lamb (1808)

'No dramatist ever used less artifice. The subjects which he chose are either taken straight from real life, or else adopted crudely from the legends of ancient Greece and Rome. In each case Heywood's manner and methods are the same. He uses simple, easy English, and sets forth unaffected feelings. The scenes have no elaborate connection. They cohere by juxtaposition. The language is never high-flown or bombastic; rarely rising to the height of poetic diction, and attaining to intensity only when the passion of the moment is overwhelming, it owes its occasional force to its sincerity.'

J. Addington Symonds (1888)

Hugh Quarshie: ARCITE

Imogen Stubbs: GAOLER'S DAUGHTER

The Two Noble Kinsmen

Henry Goodman: THOMAS KITELY

Tony Church: OLD KNO'WELL

Every Man in His Humour

Jeremy Irons: WILLMORE
Sinead Cusack: ANGELLICA BIANCA

Imogen Stubbs: HELLENA

The Rover

THE FAIR MAID OF THE WEST

THOMAS HEYWOOD

The Characters

In order of their appearance

BESS BRIDGES
SPENCER, *a gentleman in love with Bess*
CAPTAIN GOODLACK, *Spencer's friend*
FAWCETT, *another friend of Spencer's*
CARROL, *a mercenary*
TWO CAPTAINS
TWO DRAWERS
CLEM, *a vintner's apprentice*
ROUGHMAN, *a swaggerer*
A KITCHENMAID
A SURGEON
THE MAYOR OF FOY
AN ALDERMAN
AN ENGLISH MERCHANT
A SPANISH CAPTAIN
SPANISH PRISONERS
MULLISHEG, *King of Fez*
BASHAW JOFFER,   }   *his officers*
BASHAW ALCADE   }
A BANDIT CHIEF
TOTA, *Queen of Fez, wife of Mullisheg*
A FRENCH MERCHANT
AN ITALIAN MERCHANT
A PREACHER
A PORTER
A CHORUS
SERVANTS, BANDITS AND MESSENGERS

Scene One

A tavern.
Enter Clem.

CLEM.

You are welcome gentlemen. What wine will you drink? Claret, metheglin or muscadine? Cider, or perry to make you merry? Aragoose, or peter-see-peter-see-me. Canary or charnica? But, by your nose, sir, you should love a cup of malmsey: you shall have a cup of the best in Cornwall. But if you prefer the Frenchman before the Spaniard, you shall either here of the deep red grape, or the pallid white. You are a pretty tall gentleman; you should love high country wine: none but clerks and sextons love Graves wine. Oh, are you a married man, I'll furnish you with bastard, white or brown, according to the complexion of your bedfellow.

GOODLACK.

Set a pottle of sack in the fire, and carry it into the next room.

CLEM.

Score a pottle of sack in the Crown, and see at the bar for some rotten eggs, to burn it; we must have one trick or other, to vent away our bad commodities.

1ST CAPTAIN.

When puts my lord to sea?

2ND CAPTAIN.

When the wind's fair.

CARROL.

Resolve me, I entreat; can you not guess
The purpose of this voyage?

1ST CAPTAIN.

Most men think
The fleet's bound for the Islands.

CARROL.

Nay, 'tis like
The great success at Cales hath put heart
Into the English: they are all on fire
To purchase from the Spaniard. If their carracks
Come deeply laden, we shall tug them
For golden spoil.

2ND CAPTAIN.

Oh, were it come to that!

1ST CAPTAIN.

How Plymouth swells with gallants; how t'streets
Glister with gold! You cannot meet a man
But tricked in scarf and feather, that it seems
As if the pride of England's gallantry
Were harboured here. It doth appear, methinks,
A very court of soldiers.

CARROL.

It doth so.
Where shall we dine today?

2ND CAPTAIN.

Here's the best wine.

1ST CAPTAIN.

And the best wench, Bess Bridges; she's the flower.

2ND CAPTAIN.

A sweet lass, if I have any judgment.

1ST CAPTAIN.

Now, in troth,
I think she's honest.

CARROL.

Honest, and live here
What, in a public tavern! Honest, said you?

2ND CAPTAIN.

I vow she is, for me.

1ST CAPTAIN.

For all, I think.

CARROL.

Exceeding affable.

2ND CAPTAIN.

An argument
That she's not proud.

CARROL.

No; were she proud, she'd fall.

1ST CAPTAIN.

Well, she's a most attractive adamant:
Her very beauty hath upheld this house,
And gained her master much.

CARROL.

That adamant
Shall for this time draw me too: we'll dine here.

Exeunt Carrol and the Captains.

Enter Spencer.

GOODLACK.

What, to the old house still?

SPENCER.
Canst blame me, Captain?
Believe me, I was never surprised till now,
Or catched upon the sudden.

GOODLACK.
                                        Pray resolve me;
Why, being a gentleman of fortunes, means,
And well revenued, will you adventure thus
A doubtful voyage, when only such as I,
Born to no other fortunes than my sword,
Should seek abroad for pillage?

SPENCER.
                                        Pillage, Captain!
No, 'tis for honour; and the brave society
Of all these shining gallants, that attend
The great lord-general, drew me hither first,
No hope of gain or spoil.

GOODLACK.
Ay, but what draws you to this house so oft?

SPENCER.
As if thou knew'st it not.

GOODLACK.
                            What, Bess?

SPENCER.
                                    Even she.

GOODLACK.
Come, I must tell you, you forget yourself,
One of your birth and breeding thus to dote
Upon a tanner's daughter! Why, her father
Sold hides in Somersetshire and, being trade-fallen,
Sent her to service.

SPENCER.
                        Prithee speak no more;
Thou tell'st me that which I would fain forget,
Or wish I had not known. If thou wilt humour me,
Tell me she's fair and honest.

GOODLACK.
                                    Yes, and loves you.

SPENCER.
To forget that were to exclude the rest.

1ST DRAWER.
You are welcome, gentlemen. Show them into the next room
there.

2ND DRAWER.
Look out a towel, and some rolls, a salt and trenchers.

SPENCER.
No, sir, we will not dine.

2ND DRAWER.
I am sure you would if you had my stomach.
What wine drink ye, sack or claret?

SPENCER.
                                        Where's Bess?

2ND DRAWER.
Marry, above, with three or four gentlemen.

SPENCER.
Go call her.

2ND DRAWER.
I'll draw you a cup of the neatest wine in Plymouth.

SPENCER.
I'll taste none of your drawing. Go call Bess.

2ND DRAWER.
There's nothing in the mouths of these gallants but 'Bess,
Bess'.

SPENCER.
Tell her who's here.

2ND DRAWER.
The devil rid her out of the house, for me!

SPENCER.
Say y', sir?

2ND DRAWER.
Nothing but anon, anon, sir.

                                            Exit Drawers.

Enter Bess Bridges.

SPENCER.
See, she's come!

BESS.
Sweet Master Spencer, y'are a stranger grown.
Where have you been these three days?

SPENCER.
                                        The last night
I sat up late at game. Here, take this bag,
And lay't up till I call for't.
Bring some wine.

BESS.

I know your taste,
And I shall please your palate.

Exit Bess.

GOODLACK.

Troth, 'tis a pretty soul!

SPENCER.

To thee I will unbosom all my thoughts:
Were her birth but equal with her beauty,
Here would I fix my thoughts.

GOODLACK.

You are not mad, sir?
You say you love her.

SPENCER.

Never question that.

GOODLACK.

Then put her to't; win Opportunity,
She's the best bawd. If, as you say, she loves you,
She can deny you nothing.

SPENCER.

I have proved her
Unto the utmost test; examined her,
Even to a modest force; but all in vain:
She'll laugh, confer, keep company, discourse,
And something more, kiss; but beyond that compass
She no way can be drawn.

GOODLACK.

'Tis a virtue
But seldom found in taverns.

Re-enter Bess, with wine.

BESS.

'Tis of the best Graves wine, sir.

SPENCER.

Gramercy, girl: come sit.

BESS.

Pray pardon, sir, I dare not.

SPENCER.

I'll ha' it so.

BESS.

My fellows love me not, and will complain
Of such a saucy boldness.

SPENCER.

Pox on your fellows!
Sit: now, Bess, drink to me.

BESS.

To your good voyage!

She drinks.
Re-enter 2nd Drawer.

2ND DRAWER.

Did you call, sir?

SPENCER.

Yes, sir, to have your absence. Captain, this health.

GOODLACK.

Let it come, sir.

2ND DRAWER.

Must you be set, and we sait, with a – !

SPENCER.

What say you, sir?

2ND DRAWER.

Anon, anon: I come there.

Exit 2nd Drawer.

SPENCER.

What will you venture, Bess, to sea with me?

BESS.

What I love best, my heart: for I could wish
I had been born to equal you in fortune,
Or you so low, to have been ranked with me;
I could then have presumed boldly to say,
I love none but my Spencer.

SPENCER.

Bess, I thank thee.
Keep still that hundred pound 'till my return
From the Islands with my lord: If never, wench,
Take it, it is thine own.

BESS.

You bind me to you.

Re-enter 1st Drawer.

1ST DRAWER.

Bess, you must fill some wine into the portcullis;
The gentlemen there will drink none but of your drawing.

SPENCER.
She shall not rise, sir. Go, let your master snick-up.

1ST DRAWER.
And that should be first cousin to the hick-up.

Re-enter 2nd Drawer.

2ND DRAWER.
Bess, you must needs come. The gentlemen fling pots, pottles,
drawers, and all downstairs.
The whole house is in an uproar.

BESS.
Pray, pardon, sir; I needs must be gone.

3RD DRAWER.
The gentlemen swear if she come not up to them, they will
come down to her.

SPENCER.
If they come in peace,
Like civil gentlemen, they may be welcome:
If otherwise . . .

Enter Carrol and the two Captains.

CARROL.
Save you, gallants! We are somewhat bold, to press
Into your company: it may be held scarce manners;
Therefore, 'tis fit that we should crave your pardon.

SPENCER.
Sir, you are welcome; so are your friends.

1ST CAPTAIN.
                                        Some wine!

BESS.
Pray give me leave to fill it.

SPENCER.
                        You shall not stir.
So, please you, we'll join company. Drawer, more stools.

CARROL.
I take't that's a she drawer. Are you of the house?

BESS.
I am, sir.

CARROL.
        In what place?

BESS.
                        I draw.

CARROL.
Beer, do you not? You are some tapstress.

SPENCER.
Sir, the worst character you can bestow
Upon the maid is to draw wine.

CARROL.
She would draw none to us.
Perhaps she keeps a rundlet for your taste,
Which none but you must pierce.

2ND CAPTAIN.
                                I pray be civil.

SPENCER.
I know not, gentlemen, what your intents be,
Nor do I fear, or care. This is my room;
And if you bear you, as you seem in show,
Like gentlemen, sit and be sociable.

CARROL.
We will. (*To Bess:*) Minx, by your leave.
Remove, I say.

SPENCER.
                She shall not stir.

CARROL.
                        How, sir?

SPENCER.
No, sir. Could you outface the devil,
We do not fear your roaring.

CARROL.
Though you may be companion with a drudge,
It is not fit she should have place by us.
About your business, housewife.

SPENCER.
                                She is worthy
The place as the best here, and she shall keep't.

CARROL.
You lie.

They draw and justle. Carrol is slain.

GOODLACK.
The gentleman's slain: away!

BESS.
O, Heaven! What have you done?

GOODLACK.
>Undone thyself, and me too. Come away.

Exeunt Goodlack and Spencer.

Re-enter the two Drawers.

1ST DRAWER.
>One call my master, another fetch the constable.
>Here's a man killed in the room.

2ND DRAWER.
>How! A man killed, say'st thou? Is all paid?
>How fell they out, canst thou tell?

1ST DRAWER.
>Sure, about this bold Bettrice. 'Tis not so much for the death of
>the man, but how shall we come by our reckoning?

Exeunt Drawers.

BESS.
>What! Are you men, or milk-sops? Stand you still,
>Senseless as stones, and see your friend in danger
>To expire his last?

1ST CAPTAIN.
>   Tush! All our help's in vain.

2ND CAPTAIN.
>This is the fruit of whores;
>This mischief came through thee.

BESS.
>It grew first from your incivility.

1ST CAPTAIN.
>Lend me a hand, to lift his body hence.
>It was a fatal business.

Exeunt the Captains, bearing the body.

BESS.
>What shall become of me? Of all lost creatures,
>The most unfortunate. I by this
>Have lost so worthy and approved a friend.
>Whom to redeem from exile, I would give
>All that's without and in me.

Enter Fawcett.

FAWCETT.
>   Your name's Bess Bridges?

BESS.
>Your business, sir, with me?

FAWCETT.
>   Know you this ring?

BESS.
>I do: it is my Spencer's.
>I know, withal, you are his trusty friend,
>To whom he would commit it. Speak: how fares he?
>Is he in freedom, know ye?

FAWCETT.
>   He's in health
>Of body, though in mind somewhat perplexed
>For this late mischief happened.

BESS.
>   Is he fled,
>And freed from danger?

FAWCETT.
>   Neither. By this token
>He lovingly commends him to you, Bess,
>And prays you, when 'tis dark, meet him o' th' Hoe,
>Near to the new-made fort, where he'll attend you.
>He entreats you not to fail him.

BESS.
>Stand death before me; were I sure to die.
>Tell him from me, I'll come, I'll run, I'll fly.

Exeunt Bess and Fawcett.

Scene Two

The Hoe.
Enter Spencer and Captain Goodlack.

GOODLACK.
>You are too full of passion.

SPENCER.
>   Canst thou blame me,
>So sweet, so fair, so amorous and so chaste,
>And all these at an instant! Art thou sure
>Carrol is dead?

GOODLACK.
>   I can believe no less.
>You hit him in the very speeding place.

SPENCER.
>Oh! but the last of these sits near'st my heart.

GOODLACK.
    Sir, be advised by me:
    Try her, before you trust her.

SPENCER.
                            Thou counsellst well.
    I'll put her to the test and utmost trial.

Enter Bess with a bag, and Fawcett.

FAWCETT.
    I have done my message, sir.

BESS.
    Fear not, sweet Spencer; we are now alone,
    And thou art sanctuared in these mine arms.

GOODLACK.
    This place I'll guard.

FAWCETT.
                    I this.

BESS.
                        Are you not hurt,
    How is it with you?

SPENCER.
                    Bess, all my afflictions
    Are that I must leave thee: thou know'st, withal,
    I am not near my county; and to stay
    For new supply from thence might deeply engage me
    To desperate hazard.

BESS.
                        Is it coin you want?
    Here is the hundred pound you gave me of late:
    Use that, beside what I have stored and saved,
    Which makes it fifty more. Were it ten thousand,
    Nay, a whole million, Spencer, all were thine.

SPENCER.
    No; what thou hast, keep still; 'tis all thine own.
    Here be my keys: my trunks take to thy charge:
    Money, apparel, and what elsé thou findest,
    Perhaps worth my bequest and thy receiving,
    I make thee mistress of.

BESS.
                        Before, I doted;
    But now you strive to have me ecstasied.
    What would you have me do, in which to express
    my zeal to you?

SPENCER.
                I enjoin thee to keep
    Ever my picture, which in my chamber hangs:
    For when thou part'st with that, thou losest me.

BESS.
    My soul from my body may be divorced,
    But never that from me.

SPENCER.
    I have a house in Foy, a tavern called
    The Windmill; that I freely give thee, too;
    And thither, if I live, I'll send to thee.
    Time calls hence; we now must part.

BESS.
    Oh, that I had the power to make Time lame,
    I could dwell here for ever in thine arms,
    And wish it always night.

SPENCER.
    We trifle hours. Farewell!

BESS.
                        First take this ring:
    'Twas the first token of my constant love
    That passed betwixt us. When I see this next,
    And not my Spencer, I shall think thee dead;
    For, 'till death part thy body from my soul,
    I know thou wilt not part with it.

SPENCER.
    Swear for me, Bess; for thou mayst safely do't.
    Once more, farewell: at Foy thou shalt hear from me.
    I shall not live to lose thee.

FAWCETT.
                        Best be gone;
    I hear some tread.

SPENCER.
    A thousand farewells are in one contracted.

                        Exeunt Spencer and Goodlack.

BESS.
    Ha, is my Spencer gone? Oh! I shall die.

FAWCETT.
    What mean you, Bess? Will you betray your friend. Come,
    away.

                        Exeunt Bess and Fawcett.

Enter the two Drawers.

1ST DRAWER.
'Tis well that we have gotten all the money due to my master. It is the commonest thing that can be, for these captains to score and to score; but when the scores are to be paid, *non ist inventus*.

2ND DRAWER.
'Tis ordinary amongst gallants, nowadays, who had rather swear forty oaths than only this one oath – 'God, let me never be trusted!'

1ST DRAWER.
Well, howsoever, I am glad, though he killed the man, we have got our money.

Enter Bess.

BESS.
Plymouth, farewell: in Cornwall I will prove
A second fortune, and for ever mourn,
Until I see my Spencer's safe return.

Exit Bess.

2ND DRAWER.
Little knows Bess that my master hath got in these desperate debts. She hath cast up her account, and is going.

1ST DRAWER.
Whither, canst thou tell?

2ND DRAWER.
They say, to keep a tavern in Foy.

Exeunt Drawers.

Scene Three

The Windmill Tavern, Foy.
Enter Fawcett and Roughman.

FAWCETT.
In your time have you seen a sweeter creature?

ROUGHMAN.
Some week, or thereabouts.

FAWCETT.
And in that time she hath almost undone all the other taverns: the gallants make no rendezvous now but at the Windmill.

ROUGHMAN.
Spite of them, I'll have her. It shall cost me the setting on, but I'll have her.

FAWCETT.
Why, do you think she is so easily won?

ROUGHMAN.
Easily or not, I'll bid as fair and far as any man within twenty miles of my head, but I will put her to the squeak.

FAWCETT.
They say there are knights' sons already come as suitors to her.

ROUGHMAN.
'Tis like enough, some younger brothers, and so I intend to make them.

FAWCETT.
If these doings hold, she will grow rich in short time.

ROUGHMAN.
There shall be doings that shall make this Windmill my grand seat, my mansion, my palace, and my Constantinople.

Enter Bess Bridges and Clem.

FAWCETT.
Here she comes.

CLEM.
My father was a baker; and, by the report of his neighbours, as honest a man as ever lived by bread.

BESS.
And where dwelt he?

CLEM.
Below here, in the next crooked street, at the sign of the Leg. He was nothing so tall as I; but a little wee man, and somewhat huck-backed.

BESS.
I think I have heard of him.

CLEM.
Then I am sure you have heard he was an honest neighbour, and one that never loved to be meal-mouthed.

BESS.
Well, sirrah, prove an·honest servant, and you shall find me your good mistress. What company is in the Mermaid?

CLEM.
There be four sea captains. I believe they be little better than pirates, they be so flush of their ruddocks.

BESS.
No matter; they're my good customers,
And still return me profit.

CLEM.
Wot you what, mistress, how the two sailors would have served me, that called for the pound and a half of cheese?

BESS.
How was it, Clem?

CLEM.
When I brought them a reckoning, they would have had me to have scored it up. They took me for a simple gull, indeed, that would have had me to have taken chalk for cheese.

BESS.
Well, go wait upon the captains.

ROUGHMAN.
She's now at leisure: I'll go to her –
Lady, what gentlemen are those above?

BESS (*coming forward*).
 Sir, they are such as please to be my guests,
And they are kindly welcome.

ROUGHMAN.
Give me their names.

BESS.
You may go search the church-book where they were christened:
There you perhaps may learn them.

ROUGHMAN.
Minion, how!

BESS.
Pray, hands off!

ROUGHMAN.
I tell thee, maid, wife, or whate'er thou beest,
No man shall enter here but by my leave.
Come, let's be more familiar.

BESS.
'Las good man!

ROUGHMAN.
Why, knowest thou whom thou slightest? I am Roughman,
The only approved gallant of these parts,
A man of whom the roarers stand in awe,
And must not be put off.

BESS.
I never yet heard a man so praise himself.
But proved in the end a coward.

ROUGHMAN.
Coward, Bess!
You will offend me, raise in me that fury
Your beauty cannot calm. Go to; no more.

BESS.
Sir, if you thus persist to wrong my house,
Disturb my guests, and nightly domineer,
To put my friends from patience, I'll complain
And right myself before the magistrate.

ROUGHMAN.
Go to, wench:
I wish thee well; think on't, there's good for thee
Stored in my breast; and when I come in place,
I must have no man to offend mine eye:
My love can brook no rivals.

BESS.
Sir, if you come
Like other free and civil gentlemen,
You're welcome: otherwise my doors are barred you.

ROUGHMAN.
That's my good girl,
I have fortunes laid up for thee: what I have,
Command it as thine own. Go to; be wise.

BESS.
Well, I shall study for't.

ROUGHMAN.
Consider on't. Farewell.

Exeunt Roughman and Fawcett.

BESS.
What news with you?

CLEM.
I am now going to carry the captains a reckoning.

BESS.
And what's the sum?

CLEM.
Let me see – eight shillings and sixpence.

BESS.
How comes it so much?

CLEM.
Imprimis, six quarts of wine, at sevenpence the quart, seven sixpences.

BESS.
Why doest thou reckon it so?

CLEM.
Because, as they came in by hob nob, so I will bring them in a reckoning at six and at sevens.

BESS.
Well, wine, three shillings and sixpence.

CLEM.
And what wants that of ten groats?

BESS.
'Tis twopence over.

CLEM.
Then put sixpence more to it, and make it four shillings wine.

BESS.
Why so, I prithee?

CLEM.
Because of the old proverb, 'What they want in meat, let them take out in drink'. Then, for twelve pennywoth of anchoves, eighteenpence.

BESS.
How can that be?

CLEM.
Twelvepence anchoves, and sixpence oil and vinegar. Now, they shall have a saucy reckoning.

BESS.
And what for the other half-crown?

CLEM.
Bread, beer, salt, napkins, trenchers, one thing with another; so the *summa totalis* is eight shillings and sixpence.

BESS.
Well, take the reckoning from the bar.

CLEM.
What needs that? The gentlemen seem to be high-flown already. Send them in but another pottle of sack, and they will tot up the reckoning themselves. Yes, I'll about it.

Exit Clem.

BESS.
Were I not with so many suitors pestered,
And might I enjoy my Spencer, what a sweet,
Contented life were this! for money flows,
And my gain's great. But to my Roughman next.

I have a trick to try what spirit's in him.
It shall be my next business; in this passion
For my dear Spencer, I propose me this:
'Mongst many sorrows, some mirth's not amiss.

Exit Bess.

Scene Four

Fayal.
Enter Spencer and Captain Goodlack.

GOODLACK.
What were you thinking?

SPENCER.
Troth, of the world: what any man should see in't to be in love with it. Imagine that in the same instant that one forfeits all his estate, another enters upon a rich possession. As one goes to the church to be married, another is hurried to the gallows to be hanged; the last having no feeling of the first man's joy, nor the first of the last man's misery. At the same time that one lies tortured upon the rack, another lies tumbling with his mistress over head and ears in down and feathers. I cannot but wonder why any fortune should make a man ecstasied.

GOODLACK.
You give yourself too much to melancholy.

SPENCER.
These are my maxims; and were they as faithfully practised by others as truly apprehended by me, we should have less oppression, and more charity.

Enter the two Captains.

1ST CAPTAIN.
Make good thy words.

2ND CAPTAIN.
                    I say, thou hast injured me.

1ST CAPTAIN.
Tell me wherein.

2ND CAPTAIN.
                    When we assaulted Fayal,
And I had, by the general's command,
The onset, and with danger of my person
Enforced the Spaniard to a swift retreat,
And beat them from their fort, thou, when thou saw'st
All fear and danger past, madest up with me,
To share that honour which was sole mine own.

1ST CAPTAIN.
I'll prove it with my sword,
That though thou hadst the foremost place in field,
And I the second, yet my company
Was equal in the entry of the fort.

2ND CAPTAIN.
Wrong me palpably and justify the same!

SPENCER.
You shall not fight.

1ST CAPTAIN.
Why, sir, who made you first a justicer,
And taught you that word 'shall?' You are no general.

2ND CAPTAIN.
'Tis some chaplain.

1ST CAPTAIN.
                              I do not like his text.

GOODLACK.
Let's beat down their weapons.

1ST CAPTAIN.
I'll aim at him that offers to divide us!

They fight.

2ND CAPTAIN.
Pox of these part-frays! See I am wounded
By beating down my weapon.

GOODLACK.
                        How fares my friend?

SPENCER.
You sought for blood, and, gentlemen, you have it.
Let mine appease you: I am hurt to death.

1ST CAPTAIN.
My rage converts to pity, that this gentleman
Shall suffer for his goodness.

GOODLACK.
                              Noble friend,
I will revenge thy death.

SPENCER.
                  He is no friend
That murmurs such a thought. – Oh, gentlemen,
I killed a man in Plymouth, and by you
Am slain in Fayal. Heaven is just,
And will not suffer murder unrevenged.
Heaven pardon me, as I forgive you both!

Shift for yourselves: away! I say away!

1ST CAPTAIN.
Short farewells now must serve. If thou survivest,
Live to thine honour; but if thou expirest
Heaven take thy soul to mercy!

Exeunt Captains.

SPENCER.
                        I bleed much;
I must go seek a surgeon.

GOODLACK.
                        Sir, how cheer you?

SPENCER.
Like one that's bound upon a new adventure
To the other world; yet thus much, worthy friend,
The fleet is bound for England. Take your occasion
To ship yourself, and when you come to Foy,
Kindly commend me to my dearest Bess;
Thou shalt receive a will, in which I have
Possessed her of five hundred pounds a year.

GOODLACK.
A noble legacy.

SPENCER.
Only reserving a bare hundred pounds,
To see me honestly and well interred.

GOODLACK.
I shall peform your trust as carefully
As to my father.

SPENCER.
                  Mark me, Captain;
If, at thy arrival where my Bess remains,
Thou find'st her well reported, free from scandal,
My will stands firm; but if thou hear'st her branded
For loose behaviour, or immodest life,
What she should have, I here bestow on thee;
Deal faithfully betwixt my Bess and me.

GOODLACK.
Else let me die a prodigy.

SPENCER.
This ring was hers; that, be she loose or chaste,
Being her own, restore her: she will know it;
Now lead me to my chamber. O my memory!
What had I quite forgot? She hath my picture.

GOODLACK.
And what of that?

SPENCER.
If she be ranked amongst the loose and lewd,
Take it away: I hold it much indecent
A whore should ha't in keeping; but if constant,
Let her enjoy it. This my will perform.

GOODLACK.
Sense else forsake me.

SPENCER.
                    All's made even –
My peace with earth, and my atone with Heaven.

Exeunt Goodlack and Spencer.

Scene Five

A field near Foy.
Enter Bess Bridges, like a page, with a sword; and Clem.

BESS.
But that I know my mother to be chaste,
I'd swear some soldier got me.

CLEM.
It may be many a soldier's bluff jerkin came out of your father's
tan-vat.

BESS.
Methinks I have a manly spirit in me,
In this man's habit.
I could do all that I have heard discoursed.
Of Mary Ambree, or Westminster's Long Meg.

CLEM.
What Mary Ambree was I cannot tell; but unless you were
taller, you will come short of Long Meg.

BESS.
Of all thy fellows, thee I only trust,
And charge thee to be secret.

CLEM.
I am bound in my indentures to keep my master's secrets; and
should I find a man in bed with you, I would not tell.

BESS.
Begone, sir.

CLEM.
If you should swagger and kill anybody, I, being a vintner,
should be called to the bar.

Exit Clem.

BESS.
Let none condemn me of immodesty,
Because I try the courage of a man,
Who on my soul's a coward, beats my servants,
Cuffs them, and, as they pass by him, kicks my maids;
Nay, domineers over me, making himself
Lord o'er my house and household.

Enter Roughman and Fawcett.

FAWCETT.
Sir, I can now no further, weighty business calls me away.

ROUGHMAN.
Why, at your pleasure, then.
Yet I could wish that ere I passed this field,
That I could meet some Hector, so your eyes
Might witness what myself have oft repeated,
Namely, that I am valiant.

FAWCETT.
No doubt;
But now I am in haste. Farewell.

Exit Fawcett.

ROUGHMAN.
How many times brave words bear out a man!
For if he can but make a noise, he's feard,
To talk of frays, although he ne'er had heart.
To face a man in the field, that's a brave fellow.
I have been valiant, I must needs confess,
In street and tavern, where there have been men
Ready to part the fray; but for the fields,
They are too cold to fight in.

BESS.
You are a villain and a coward; and you lie.

She strikes him.

ROUGHMAN.
You wrong me, I protest. Sweet, courteous gentleman,
I never did you wrong.

BESS.
                    Wilt tell me that?
Draw forth thy coward sword, and suddenly,

Or, as I am a man, I'll run thee through,
And leave thee dead i' the field.

ROUGHMAN.
                              Hold! as you are a gentleman.
I have ta'en an oath I will not fight today.

BESS.
Th'ast took a blow already, and the lie:
Will not both these enrage thee?

ROUGHMAN.
No; would you give the bastinado too,
I will not break mine oath.

BESS.
                              Oh! Your name's Roughman:
No day doth pass you but that you hurt or kill!
Is this out of your calender?

ROUGHMAN.
                              I! You are deceived.
I ne'er drew sword in anger, I protest,
Unless it were upon some poor, weak fellow,
That ne'er wore steel about him.

BESS.
                                        Throw your sword.

ROUGHMAN.
Here, sweet young sir;

He gives up his sword.

                              But as you are a gentleman,
Do not impair mine honour.

BESS.
                                        Tie that shoe.

ROUGHMAN.
I shall, sir.

BESS.
                              Untruss that point.

ROUGHMAN.
Anything, this day, to save mine oath.

BESS.
Enough; – yet not enough. Lie down,
'Till I stride o'er thee.

ROUGHMAN.
                              Sweet sir, anything.

BESS.
Rise, thou hast leave. Now, Roughman, thou art blest;
This day thy life is saved; look to the rest.
Take back thy sword.

ROUGHMAN.
Oh! you are generous: honour me so much
As let me know to whom I owe my life.

BESS.
I am Bess Bridges' brother.

ROUGHMAN.
                              Still methought
That you were something like her.

BESS.
                              I have heard
You domineer and revel in her house,
Control her servants, and abuse her guests,
Which if I ever shall hereafter hear,
Thou art but a dead man.

ROUGHMAN.
She never told me of a brother living;
But you have power to sway me.

BESS.
But for I see you are a gentleman,
I am content this once to let you pass;
But if I find you fall into relapse
The second's far more dangerous.

ROUGHMAN.
                              I shall fear it.
Sir, will you take the wine?

BESS.
                              I am for London,
And for these two terms cannot make return;
But if you see my sister, you may say
I was in health.

                                        Exit Bess.

ROUGHMAN (*aside*).
                              Too well: the devil take you!
None saw't: he's gone for London; I am unhurt;
Then who shall publish this disgrace abroad?
One man's no slander, should he speak his worst.
My tongue's as loud as his; but in this country
Both of more fame and credit. Should we contest,
I can outface the proudest. This is, then, my comfort.

Roughman, thou art still the same,
For a disgrace not seen is held no shame.

Exit Roughman.

Scene Six

Fayal.
Enter two sailors.

1ST SAILOR.
Aboard! aboard! the wind stands fair for England:
The ships have all weighed anchor.

2ND SAILOR.
A stiff gale
Blows from the shore.

Enter Captain Goodlack.

GOODLACK.
The sailors call aboard, and I am forced
To leave my friend now at the point of death,
And cannot close his eyes.

2ND SAILOR.
Aboard, aboard!

1ST SAILOR.
Sir, will you take the long-boat and aboard?

Enter a third Sailor.

GOODLACK.
With all my heart.

3RD SAILOR.
What, are you ready, mates?

1ST SAILOR.
We stayed for you. Thou canst not tell who's dead?
The great bell rung out now.

3RD SAILOR.
They say 'twas for one Spencer, who this night
Died of a mortal wound.

GOODLACK.
My worthy friend:
– Was his name Spencer?

3RD SAILOR.
Yes, sir, a gentleman of good account,
And well known in the Navy.

GOODLACK.
This is the end of all mortality.
It will be news unpleasing to his Bess.
Now may I find yon tanner's daughter turned
Unchaste or wanton, I shall gain by it.
Here is the will. Five hundred pounds a year.
I cannot fare amiss, but long to see
Whether these lands belong to her or me.

Exeunt omnes.

Enter Spencer and Surgeon.

SURGEON.
Nay, fear not, sir: now you have escaped this dressing,
My life for yours.

SPENCER.
I thank thee, honest friend.

SURGEON.
There is a gentleman, one of your name,
That died within this hour.

SPENCER.
My name! What was he? Of what sickness died he?

SURGEON.
No sickness, but a slight hurt in the body,
Which showed at first no danger, but, being searched,
He died at the third dressing.

SPENCER.
That hundred pound I had prepared to expend
Upon mine own expected funeral,
I for name's-sake will now bestow on his.

SURGEON.
A noble resolution.

SPENCER.
What ships are bound for England?
I would gladly venture to sea, though weak.

SURGEON.
All bound that way are under sail already.

SPENCER.
Here's no security;
For when the beaten Spaniards shall return,
They'll spoil whom they can find.

SURGEON.
We have a ship,
A London merchant, now bound for Mamorah,

A town in Barbary; please you to use that,
You shall command a free passage: ten months hence,
We hope to visit England.

SPENCER.
Friend, I thank thee.

SURGEON.
I'll bring you to the master, who I know will entertain you
gladly.

SPENCER.
When I have seen the funeral rites performed
To the dead body of my countryman
And kinsman, I will take your courteous offer
Bess, no doubt, will hear news of my death;
On her behaviour I will build my fate,
There raise my love, or thence erect my hate.

Exeunt Spencer and Surgeon.

Scene Seven

Foy. The Windmill Tavern.
Enter Roughman.

ROUGHMAN.
Where be these drawers – rascals, I should say –
That will give no attendance.

Enter Fawcett.

CLEM.
Anon, anon, sir.

ROUGHMAN.
Oh! You're well met. Just as I prophesied,
So it fell out.

FAWCETT.
As how, I pray?

ROUGHMAN.
Had you but stayed the crossing of one field,
You had beheld a Hector, the boldest Trojan
That ever Roughman met with.

FAWCETT.
Pray, what was he?

ROUGHMAN.
You talk of Little Davy, Cutting Dick,
And divers such; but tush! this hath no fellow.

FAWCETT.
Of what stature and years was he?

ROUGHMAN.
Indeed, I must confess he was no giant,
Nor above fifty; but he did bestir him –
Was here, and there, and everywhere, at once,
That I was ne'er so put to't since the midwife
First wrapped my head in linen. Where is Bess?

CLEM.
What, you here, again! Now we shall have such roaring!

ROUGHMAN.
You, sirrah, call your mistress.

CLEM.
Yes, sir, I know it is my duty to call her mistress.

ROUGHMAN.
Shall we have humours, sauce-box? You have ears;
I'll teach you prick-song.

CLEM.
I will call her.

ROUGHMAN.
Do, sir; you had best.

CLEM.
If you were twenty Roughmans, if you lug me by the ears again,
I'll draw!

ROUGHMAN.
Ha! what will you draw?

CLEM.
The best wine in the house for your worship; but I can assure
you that she is either not stirring, or else not in case.

ROUGHMAN.
How not in case?

CLEM.
I think she hath not her smock on; for I think I saw it lie at her
bed's head.

ROUGHMAN.
What! Drawers grow capricious?

CLEM.
Help! Help!

Enter Bess Bridges.

BESS.
What uproar's this? Shall we be never rid
From these disturbances?

ROUGHMAN.
                    Why, how now, Bess?
Is this your housewifery? When you are mine,
I'll have you rise as early as the lark.
Look to the bar yourself; these lazy rascals
Will bring your state behind hand.

CLEM.
You lie, sir.

ROUGHMAN.
How! lie.

CLEM.
Yes, sir, at the Raven in the High Street. I was at your lodging
this morning.

ROUGHMAN.
You will about your business: must you here stand gaping and
idle?

Roughman strikes Clem.

BESS.
You wrong me, sir.
And tyrannize too much over my servants.
I will have no man touch them but myself.

CLEM.
If I do not put ratsbane into his wine –

                                    Exit Clem.

ROUGHMAN.
What! rise at noon?
A man may fight a tall fray in a morning,
Be hacked in mangled pieces, and you fast,
Close in your bed, ne'er dream on't.

BESS.
Fought you this day?

ROUGHMAN.
And ne'er was better put to't in my days.

BESS.
I pray, how was't?

ROUGHMAN.
Thus. As I passed yon fields –

Enter Kitchenmaid.

MAID.
I pray, forsooth, what shall I reckon for the jowl of ling in the
portcullis?

ROUGHMAN.
A pox upon your jowls, you kitchen-stuff!
Go, scour your skillets, pots, and dripping-pans,
And interrupt not us.

He kicks at her.

MAID.
The devil take your ox-heels, you foul cod's-head! must you be
kicking!

ROUGHMAN.
Minion! dare you scold?

MAID.
Yes, sir; and lay my ladle over your coxcomb.

                                    Exit Kitchenmaid.

BESS.
I do not think that thou darest strike a man
That swagger'st thus o'er women.

ROUGHMAN.
How now, Bess?

BESS.
Shall we be never quiet?

FAWCETT.
You are too rude.

ROUGHMAN.
Now I profess all patience.

BESS.
Then proceed.

ROUGHMAN.
Rising up early, minion, whilst you slept,
To cross yon field, I had but newly parted
With this my friend, but that I soon espied
A gallant fellow, and most strongly armed:
In the mid-field we met, and, both being resolute,
We justled for the wall.

BESS.
Why, did there stand a wall in the mid-field?

ROUGHMAN.
I meant, strove for the way.
Two such brave spirits meeting, straight both drew.

Re-enter Clem.

CLEM.
The maid, forsooth, sent me to know whether you would have
the shoulder of mutton roasted or sod?

ROUGHMAN.
A mischief on your shoulders!

Roughman strikes Clem.

BESS.
You heap wrongs on wrongs.

ROUGHMAN.
                              I was in fury,
To think upon the violence of that fight,
And could not stay my rage.

FAWCETT.
                    Once more proceed.

ROUGHMAN.
Oh! Had you seen two tilting meteors justle
In the mid-region, with like fear and fury
We too encountered.
Blows came about my head – I took them still;
Thrusts by my sides, 'twixt my body and my arms –
Yet still I put them by.

BESS.
When they were past, he put them by. – Go on.
But in this fury, what happened of him?

ROUGHMAN.
I think I paid him home: he's soundly mauled.
I bosomed him at every second thrust.

BESS.
Scaped he with life?

ROUGHMAN.
Ay, that's my fear. If he recover this,
I'll never trust my sword more.

BESS.
Why fly you not, if he be in such danger?

ROUGHMAN.
Because a witch once told me
I ne'er should die for murder.

BESS.
I believe thee.
But tell me, pray, was not this gallant fellow

A pretty, fair, young youth, about my years?

ROUGHMAN.
Even thereabout.

CLEM.
He was not fifty, then?

BESS.
Much of my stature?

ROUGHMAN.
Much about your pitch.

CLEM.
He was no giant, then?

BESS.
And wore a suit like this?

ROUGHMAN.
I half suspect.

BESS.
                    That gallant fellow,
So mangled and wounded, was myself.
You base, white-livered slave! it was this shoe
That you stooped to untie; untrussed those points;
And, like a beastly coward, lay along
Till I strid over thee. Speak; was't not so?

ROUGHMAN.
It cannot be denied.

BESS.
Hare-hearted fellow! Milksop! Dost not blush?
Give me that rapier: I will make thee swear
Thou shalt redeem this scorn thou hast incurred,
Or in this woman shape I'll cudgel thee,
And beat thee through the streets. As I am Bess, I'll do't.

ROUGHMAN.
Hold, hold! I swear.

BESS.
Dare not to enter at my door till then.

ROUGHMAN.
Shame confounds me quite.

BESS.
That shame redeem, perhaps we'll do thee grace;
I love the valiant, but despise the base.

                                                Exit.

CLEM.
Will you be kicked, sir?

ROUGHMAN.
                    She hath wakened me,
And kindled that dead fire of courage in me
Which all this while hath slept. To spare my flesh,
And wound my fame, what is't? I will not rest,
'Til by some valiant deed I have made good
All my disgraces past. I'll cross the street,
And strike the next brave fellow that I meet.

FAWCETT.
I am bound to see the end on't.

ROUGHMAN.
                    Are you sir?

Roughman beats off Fawcett.
Exeunt Omnes.

Scene Eight

A street in Foy.
Enter the Mayor of Foy, an Alderman, and Servant.
A shot within.

ALDERMAN.
'Twas said a ship is now put into harbour:
Know whence she is.

SERVANT.
                    I'll bring news from the quay.

Exit Servant.

MAYOR.
Believe me sir, she bears herself so well,
No man can justly blame her; and I wonder,
Being a single woman as she is,
And living in a house of such resort,
She is no more distasted.

ALDERMAN.
The best gentlemen
The country yields become her daily guests.
Sure, sir, I think she's rich.

MAYOR.
Thus much I know: would I could buy her state,
Were't for a brace of thousands!
To tell you true, sir, I could wish a match

Betwixt her and mine own and only son;
And stretch my purse, too, upon that condition.

ALDERMAN.
Please you, I'll motion it.

Re-enter Servant.

SERVANT.
One of the ships is new come from the Islands;
The greatest man of note's one Captain Goodlack.
It is but a small vessel.

Enter Captain Goodlack and Sailors.

GOODLACK.
I'll meet you straight at the Windmill.
Not one word of my name.

1ST SAILOR.
We understand you.

MAYOR.
Pray, sir, the news from thence?

GOODLACK.
The best is, that the general is in health,
And Fayal won from the Spaniards; but the fleet,
Extremely weather-beaten. You, sir, I take it,
Are mayor o' the town.

MAYOR.
                    I am the King's lieutenant.

GOODLACK.
I have some letters of import from one,
A gentleman of very good account,
That died late in the Islands, to a maid
That keeps a tavern here.

MAYOR.
                    Her name Bess Bridges?

GOODLACK.
The same. I was desired to make inquiry
What fame she bears, and what reports she's of.
Now, you, sir, being her chief magistrate,
Can best resolve me.

MAYOR.
                    To our understanding
She's without stain or blemish, well reputed;
And hath won the love of all.

GOODLACK (*aside*).
                    The worse for me.

ALDERMAN.
>I can assure you, many narrow eyes
>Have looked on her and her condition;
>But those that with most envy have endeavoured
>To entrap her, have returned, won by her virtues.

GOODLACK.
>I am glad to hear't. Sir, I have now some business.

MAYOR.
>I entreat you to sup with me tonight.

ALDERMAN.
>Sir, I may trouble you.

Exeunt Mayor and Alderman.

GOODLACK.
>Five hundred pound a year out of my way,
>Is there no flaw that I can tax her with,
>To forfeit this revenue? Is she such a saint,
>None can missay her? Why, then, I myself
>Will undertake it. If in her demeanour
>I can find but one blemish, stain or spot,
>It is five hundred pound a year well got.

Exeunt Goodlack and Sailors.

Scene Nine

The Windmill Tavern.
>*Enter Clem and Sailors on one side: on the other, Roughman, who draws and beats them off; then re-enter Clem, and the Sailors with Bess.*

BESS.
>But did he fight it bravely?

CLEM.
>I assure you, mistress, most dissolutely: he hath run this sailor three times through the body, and yet never touched his skin.

BESS.
>How can that be?

CLEM.
>Through the body of his doublet, I meant.

BESS.
>How shame, base imputation and disgrace,
>Can make a coward valiant! Sirrah, you look to the bar.

Exit Clem.

>I understand you came now from the Islands?

1ST SAILOR.
>We did so.

BESS.
>If you can tell me tidings of one gentleman,
>I shall require you largely.

1ST SAILOR.
>Of what name?

BESS.
>One Spencer.

1ST SAILOR.
>We both saw and knew the man.

BESS.
>Only for that, call for what wine you please.
>Pray tell me where you left him?

2ND SAILOR.
>In Fayal.

BESS.
>Was he in health? How did he fare?

2ND SAILOR.
>Why, well.

BESS.
>For that good news, spend, revel, and carouse;
>Your reckoning's paid beforehand. – I am ecstasied. –
>You told me he was well; shall I not rejoice?

1ST SAILOR.
>He's well, in heaven; for, mistress, he is dead.

BESS.
>Ha! Dead! Was't so you said? Th' hast given me, friend,
>But one wound yet: speak but that word again,
>And kill me outright.

2ND SAILOR.
>He lives not.

BESS.
>And shall I? – Wilt thou not break, heart?
>Are these my ribs wrought out of brass or steel,
>Thou canst not craze their bars?

1ST SAILOR.
>Mistress, use patience.

BESS.
You advise well.
Pray take the best room in the house, and there call for what
wine best tastes you:

Exeunt Sailors.

That it should be my fate! Poor sweetheart!
I do but think how thou becom'st thy grave,
In which would I lay by thee.

Enter Goodlack.

(*Aside.*) It cannot, sure, be true
That he is dead: Death could not be so envious,
To snatch him in his prime. I study to forget
That'er was such a man.

GOODLACK (*aside*).
If not impeach her,
My purpose is to seek to marry her.
If she deny me, I'll conceal the will,
Or, at the least, make her compound for half –
Save you, (*To Bess*:) fair gentlewoman.

BESS.
You are welcome, sir.

GOODLACK.
I hear say there's a whore here, that draws wine.
I am sharp set, and newly come from sea,
And I would see the trash.

BESS.
Sure, you mistake, sir.
If you desire attendance and some wine,
I can command you both. – Where be these boys?

GOODLACK.
Are you the mistress?

BESS.
I command the house.

GOODLACK.
Of what birth are you, pray?

BESS.
A tanner's daughter.

GOODLACK.
Where born?

BESS.
In Somersetshire.

GOODLACK.
A trade-fallen tanner's daughter go so brave!
Oh! You have tricks to compass these gay clothes.

BESS.
None, sir, but what are honest.

GOODLACK.
What's your name?

BESS.
Bess Bridges most men call me.

GOODLACK.
Y'are a whore.

BESS.
Sir, I will fetch you wine, to wash your mouth;
It is so foul, I fear't may fester, else:
There may be danger in't.

GOODLACK.
How's this, you baggage.

BESS.
Good, sir, at this time I am scarce myself,
By reason of a great and weighty loss
That troubles me.

GOODLACK.
Y'are a strumpet.

BESS.
Pardon, sir!
I both must and will leave you.

Exit Bess.

GOODLACK.
Did not this well? This will stick in my stomach.
I could repent my wrongs done to this maid;
But I'll not leave her thus; if she still love him,
I'll break her heart-strings with some false report
Of his unkindness. Speak: where's your mistress?

CLEM.
Gone up to her chamber.

Scene Ten

A bedroom in the tavern.
Enter Bess, with Spencer's picture

BESS.

To die, and not vouchsafe some few commends
Before his death, was most unkindly done.
This picture is more courteous: 'twill not shrink
For twenty thousand kisses.

Enter Captain Goodlack.

GOODLACK.

Where's this harlot?

BESS.

You are immodest, sir, to press thus rudely into my private
chamber.

GOODLACK.

Pox of modesty.
When punks must have it mincing in their mouths! –
And have I found thee? Thou shalt hence with me.

He seizes the picture.

BESS.

Rob me not of the chiefest wealth I have;
Search all my trunks; take all the coin I have
So I may keep that still.

GOODLACK.

Think'st thou that bribes
Can make me leave my friend's will unperformed?

BESS.

What was that friend?

GOODLACK.

One Spencer, dead i' the Islands,
Whose very last words, uttered at his death,
Were these: 'If ever thou shalt come to Foy,
Take thence my picture, and deface it quite;
For let it not be said, my portraiture
Shall grace a strumpet's chamber.'

BESS.

You lie! You are a villain! 'Twas not so.
'Tis more than sin thus to belie the dead.
He knew, if ever I would have transgressed,
'T had been with him: he durst have sworn me chaste,
And died in that belief.

GOODLACK.

Are you so brief?
Nay, I'll not trouble you. God be wi' you!

BESS.

Are you a Christian?
Have you any name that ever good man gave you?
'Twas no saint you were called after. What's thy name?

GOODLACK.

My name is Captain Thomas Good –

BESS.

I see no good in thee: rase that syllable out of thy name.

GOODLACK.

Goodlack's my name.

BESS.

I cry you mercy, sir: I now remember you;
You were my Spencer's friend: I will not wrong the dead.
But if it was his will you take this hence
For his sake I entreat –

GOODLACK.

I am inexorable.

BESS.

I may but take my leave on't.

GOODLACK.

You'll return it?

BESS.

As I am chaste, I will.

Goodlack returns the picture.

Thou resemblest him
For whose sweet safety I was every morning
Down on my knees, and with the lark's sweet tunes
I did begin my prayers; and when sad sleep
Had charmed all eyes, when none save the bright stars
Were up and waking, I remembered thee;
But all, all to no purpose. Take one sweet kiss,
As my last farewell. I am resolv'd.
This picture sir, and all that's left of him
I do restore thee back.

GOODLACK.

My Mistress Bess,
I have better tidings for you.

BESS.

You will restore my picture? Will you?

GOODLACK.

Yes, and more than that:

This ring from my friend's finger, sent to you
With infinite commends.

BESS.

You change my blood.

GOODLACK.

These writings are the evidence of lands:
Five hundred pound a year's bequeathed to you,
Of which I here possess you: all is yours.

BESS.

Then my Spencer, he is dead indeed.

GOODLACK.

I tell you true.

Bess swoons and falls.

BESS.

This surplusage of love hath made my loss,
That was but great before, now infinite –

GOODLACK.

Sweet Mistress Bess, will you command my service?

BESS.

Four thousand pound, beside this legacy,
In jewels, gold, and silver, I can make,
And every man discharged.

GOODLACK.

What study you?

BESS.

It may be compassed. There's in this my purpose
No impossibility.
I will impart a secret to your trust,
Which, saving you, no mortal should partake.

GOODLACK.

Both for his love and yours, command my service.

BESS.

There's a prize
Brought into Falmouth road, a good tight vessel;
The bottom will but cost eight hundred pound;
You shall have money: buy it.

GOODLACK.

To what end?

BESS.

That you shall know hereafter. Furnish her
With all provision needful: spare no cost;
And join with you a ging of lusty lads,

Such as will bravely man her. All the charge
I will commit to you; and when she's fitted,
Captain, she is thine own.

GOODLACK.

I sound it not.
If to succeed your Spencer in his love,
I would expose me wholly to your wishes.

BESS.

Alas! my love sleeps with him in his grave,
And cannot thence be wakened: yet for his sake
Spare me the rest. – This voyage I intend,
Though some may blame, all lovers will commend.

Exeunt Goodlack and Bess.

Scene Eleven

On board a Spanish vessel.
    *After an alarum, enter a Spanish Captain with Sailors, bringing in an
English Merchant, Spencer and the Surgeon, prisoners.*

SPANISH CAPTAIN.

For Fayal's loss and spoil, by the English done,
We are in part revenged. There's not a vessel
That bears upon her top St George's cross,
But for that act shall suffer.

MERCHANT.

Insult not, Spaniard,
Nor be too proud, that thou by odds of ships,
Provision, men and powder madest us yield.
Had you come one to one, then we by this
Had made the carcase of your ship your graves.

SPANISH CAPTAIN.

Englishman, thy ship shall yield us pillage.
These prisoners we will keep in strongest hold,
To pay no other ransom than their lives.

SPENCER.

Degenerate Spaniard, there's no noblesse in thee,
To threaten men unarmed and miserable.
Thou mightest as well tread o'er a field of slaughter,
And kill them o'er that are already slain,
And brag thy manhood.

SPANISH CAPTAIN.

Sirrah, what are you?

SPENCER.
Thy equal, as I am a prisoner;
But once, to stay a better man than thou,
A gentleman in my country.

SPANISH CAPTAIN.
We have strappados, bolts,
And engines, to the mainmast fastened,
Can make you gentle.

SPENCER.
                    Spaniard, do thy worst:
Thou canst not act more tortures than my courage
Is able to endure.

SPANISH CAPTAIN.
These Englishmen, nothing can daunt them. Even in misery,
they'll not regard their masters.

SPENCER.
Master! Insulting, bragging Thrasos!

SPANISH CAPTAIN.
His sauciness we'll punish 'bove the rest;
About their censures we will next devise.
And now towards Spain, with our brave English prize.

                              Flourish. Exeunt omnes.

Scene Twelve

The Windmill Tavern.
Enter Bess, the Mayor of Foy, Alderman, and Clem.

BESS.
A table and some stools!

CLEM.
I shall give you occasion to ease your tails presently.

Tables and stools are set out.

BESS.
Will't please you sit?

MAYOR.
With all our hearts, and thank you.

BESS.
Fetch me that parchment in my closet window.

ALDERMAN.
And now you are alone, fair Mistress Elizabeth

I think it good to taste you with a motion
That no way can displease you.

BESS.
                              Pray, speak on.

ALDERMAN.
'T hath pleased here Master Mayor so far to look
Into your fair demeanour, that he thinks you a fit match for his
son.

Re-enter Clem, with the parchment.

CLEM.
Here's Susannah betwixt the two wicked elders.

BESS.
About your business.

CLEM.
Here's the parchment; but if it be the lease of your house, I can
assure you 'tis out.

BESS.
The years are not expired.

CLEM.
No; it is out of your closet.

                              Exit Clem.

ALDERMAN.
What think you, Mistress Elzabeth?

BESS.
Sir, I thank you; Marry, gentle sir!
'Las, I have sadder business now in hand
Than sprightly marriage. Pray read there.

MAYOR (*reads*).
'The last will and testament of Elzabeth Bridges;
To be committed to the trust of the mayor and aldermen of Foy,
and their successors for ever.
To set up young beginners in their trade, a thousand pound.
To relieve such as have had loss by sea, five hundred pound.
To every maid that's married out of Foy, whose name's
Elzabeth, ten pound.
To relieve maimed soldiers, by the year, ten pound.
To Captain Goodlack, if he shall perform the business
He's employed in, five hundred pound.
The legacies for Spencer thus to stand:
To number all the poorest of his kin.'

BESS.
Enough! You see, sir, I am now too poor

To bring a dowry with me fit for your son.

MAYOR.
You want a precedent, you so abound in charity and goodness.

BESS.
All my servants I leave at your discretions to dipose;
Not one but I have left some legacy.
What shall become of me, or what I purpose;
Spare further to inquire.

MAYOR.
We'll take our leaves, and prove to you faithful executors in this
bequest.

ALDERMAN.
Let never such despair,
As, dying rich, shall make the poor their heir.

Exeunt Mayor and Alderman.

BESS.
Why, what is all the wealth the world contains, without my
Spencer?

Enter Roughman and Fawcett.

ROUGHMAN.
Where's my sweet Bess?
Shall I become a welcome suitor, now
That I have changed my copy?

BESS.
I'll find employment for you.

Enter Captain Goodlack, Sailors and Clem.

GOODLACK.
A gallant ship, and wondrous proudly trimmed;
Well-caulked, well-tackled, every way prepared.

BESS.
Here, then, our mourning for a season end.

ROUGHMAN.
Bess, shall I strike that captain? Say the word,
I'll have him by the ears.

BESS.
Not for the world.

GOODLACK.
What saith that fellow?

BESS.
He desires your love, good Captain: let him ha' it.

GOODLACK.
Then change a hand.

BESS.
I am bound upon a voyage:
Will you, in this adventure, take such part
As I myself shall do?

ROUGHMAN.
With my fair Bess.
To the world's end.

BESS.
Then, captain and lieutenant both join hands;
Such are your places now.

GOODLACK.
We two are friends.

BESS.
I next must swear you two, with all your ging,
True to some articles you must observe,
Reserving to myself a prime command,
Whilst I enjoin nothing unreasonable.

GOODLACK.
All this is granted.

BESS.
Then, first you said your ship was trim and gay:
I'll have her pitched all o'er, no spot of white,
No colour to be seen: no sail but black;
No flag but sable.

GOODLACK.
'Twill be ominous,
And bode disastrous fortune.

BESS.
I will ha't so.

GOODLACK.
Why, then, she shall be pitched black as the devil.

BESS.
She shall be called the *Negro*.

ROUGHMAN.
But wither are we bound?

BESS.
Pardon me that:
When we are out at sea, I'll tell you all.
For mine own wearing I have rich apparel,
For man or woman, as occasion serves.

CLEM.
> But, mistress, if you be going to sea, what shall become of me
> a-land?

BESS.
> I'll give thee thy full time.

CLEM.
> Shall I stay here to score a pudding in the Half-Moon, and see
> my mistress at the mainyard, with her sails up and spread? No;
> it shall be seen that my teeth are as strong to grind biscuit as the
> best sailor of them all, and my stomach as able to digest
> powdered beef and poor-john.

BESS.
> If thou hast so much courage, the captain shall accept thee.

CLEM.
> If I have so much courage! When did you see a little fellow
> without a tall stomach? I doubt not but to prove an honour to all
> the potboys in Cornwall.

GOODLACK.
> What now remains?

FAWCETT.
> To make myself associate
> In this bold enterprise.

GOODLACK.
> Most gladly, sir.
> And now our number's full, what's to be done?

BESS.
> First, set the cellars ope, that these my mates
> May quaff unto the health of our boon voyage,
> Our needful things being once conveyed abroad;
> Then, casting up our caps, in sign of joy,
> Our purpose is to bid farewell to Foy.

> *Exeunt all. Hautboys long.*

Scene Thirteen

On board the 'Negro'.
> *Enter Bess as a sea captain, Captain Goodlack, Roughman and
> others.*

BESS.
> Good morrow, Captain. Oh, this last sea fight
> Was gallantly performed! It did me good
> To see the Spanish carvel vail her top

Unto my maiden flag. Where ride we now?

GOODLACK.
> Among the islands.
> Attend me, good Lieutenant; and, sweet Bess,
> With ten tall fellows I have manned our boat,
> To see what straggling Spaniards they can take.

BESS.
> What coast is this we now descry from far?

GOODLACK.
> Yon fort's called Fayal.

BESS.
> Is that the place where Spencer's body lies?

GOODLACK.
> Yes; in yon church he's buried.

BESS.
> Then know, to this place was my voyage bound,
> To fetch the body of my Spencer thence;
> In his own country to erect a tomb
> And lasting monument, where, when I die,
> In the same bed of earth my bones may lie.
> Yours be the spoil, he mine: I crave no more.
> Then, all that love me, arm and make for shore.

ROUGHMAN.
> May that man die derided and accursed
> That will not follow where a woman leads.

GOODLACK.
> Roughman, you are too rash, and counsel ill.
> Have not the Spaniards fortified the town?
> In all our ging we are but sixty-five.

ROUGHMAN.
> Come, I'll make one.

GOODLACK.
> See where Fawcett is returned with prisoners.

> *Enter Fawcett with two Spaniards.*

FAWCETT.
> These Spaniards we by break of day surprised,
> As they were ready to take boat for fishing.

GOODLACK.
> Spaniards, upon your lives, resolve us truly,
> How strong's the town and fort?

1ST SPANIARD.
> Since English Raleigh won and spoiled it first,
> The town's re-edified, and fort new built,
> And four field-pieces in the block-house lie,
> To keep the harbour's mouth.

GOODLACK.
> And what's one ship to these?

BESS.
> Was there not, in the time of their abode,
> A gentleman called Spencer buried there,
> Within the church, whom some report was slain,
> Or perished by a wound?

1ST SPANIARD.
>   Indeed, there was,
> But when the English Navy were sailed thence,
> And that the Spaniards did possess the town,
> Because they held him for a heretic,
> They straight removed his body from the church.

BESS.
> And would the tyrants be so uncharitable
> To wrong the dead! Where did they then bestow him?

1ST SPANIARD.
> They buried him i' the fields.

BESS.
>   Oh, still more cruel!

1ST SPANIARD.
> The man that owned the field, doubtful his corn
> Would never prosper whilst a heretic's body
> Lay there, he made a petition to the church
> To ha' it digged up and burnt; and so it was.

BESS.
> What's he, that loves me, would persuade me to live,
> Not rather leap o'er hatches into the sea?
> Yet ere I die, I hope to be revenged
> Upon some Spaniards, for my Spencer's wrong.

ROUGHMAN.
> Let's first begin with these.

BESS.
> 'Las, these poor slaves. Besides their pardoned lives,
> One give them money.
> Command the gunner fire upon the fort.

ROUGHMAN.
> And if he can to batter it to earth.

BESS.
> Pray for Bess Bridges, and speak well o' the English.

1ST & 2ND SPANIARDS.
> We shall.

> *A gun is discharged.*
> *Enter Clem, falling through haste.*

CLEM.
> A sail! A sail!

BESS.
> From whence?

CLEM.
> A pox upon yon gunner! Could he not give warning before he
> had shot?

ROUGHMAN.
> Why, I prithee?

CLEM.
> Why? I was sent to the top-mast, to watch, and there I fell fast
> asleep. Bounce! quoth the guns; down tumbles Clem; and, if by
> chance my feet had not hung in the tackles, you must have sent
> to England for a bone-setter.

ROUGHMAN.
> Thou told'st us of a sail.

> *Enter Sailor, above.*

SAILOR.
> Arm, gentlemen! a gallant ship of war
> Makes with her full sails this way; who, it seems,
> Hath took a bark of England.

BESS.
>   Which we'll rescue,
> Or perish in the adventure. You have sworn
> That, whosoe'er we conquer or miscarry,
> Not to reveal my sex.

ALL.
> We have.

BESS.
> Then, for your country's honour, my revenge,
> For your own fame, and hope of golden spoil,
> Stand bravely to't. – The manage of the fight we leave to you.

GOODLACK.
> Then, now up with your fights, and let your ensigns,
> Blest with St George's cross, play with the winds. –

Fair Bess, keep you your cabin.

BESS.

Captain, you wrong me: I will face the fight;
And where the bullets sing loud'st 'bout mine ears,
There shall you find me cheering up my men.

ROUGHMAN.

This wench would of a coward make a Hercules.

BESS.

Trumpets, a charge! And with your whistles shrill,
Sound, boatswains, an alarum to your mates.
The whilst the thundering ordnance bear the bass.

GOODLACK.

To fight against the Spaniards we desire.
Alarum trumpets!

Alarum.

ROUGHMAN.

Gunners, straight give fire!

Exeunt.

A shot is fired. Battle.
  Re-enter Captain Goodlack, wounded, Bess, Roughman,
Fawcett and Clem.

GOODLACK.

I am shot, and can no longer man the deck:
Yet let not my wound daunt your courage, mates.

BESS.

For every drop of blood that thou hast shed,
I'll have a Spaniard's life. – Advance your targets,
And now cry all, 'Board! Board! Amain for England!'

Alarum: exeunt Goodlack, Bess, etc.
Re-enter Bess, Roughman, Fawcett, Clem etc. victorious.

The Spaniards are their prisoners.

How is it with the Captain?

ROUGHMAN.

                    Nothing dangerous;
But, being shot i' the thigh, he keeps his cabin,
And cannot rise to greet your victory.

BESS.

He stood it bravely out, whilst he could stand.

CLEM.

But for these Spaniards, now, you Don Diegos.

ROUGHMAN.

Before we further censure them, let's know what English
prisoners they have here aboard.

Exit Roughman.

1ST SPANIARD.

You may command them all. We that were now lords over
them, fortune hath made slaves.
Release our prisoners.

BESS.

Had my captain died,
Not one proud Spaniard had escaped with life.
Your ship is forfeit to us, and your goods:
So live. – Give him his long boat: him and his
Set safe ashore; and pray for English Bess.

1ST SPANIARD.

I know not whom you mean; but be't your queen,
Famous Elizabeth, I shall report she and her subjects are both
merciful.

Exeunt Spaniards.
Re-enter Roughman, with a Merchant, Spencer, and English
Prisoners.

BESS.

Whence are you sir, and whither were you bound?

MERCHANT.

I am a London merchant, bound for Barbary: but by this
Spanish man-of-war surprised,
Pillaged and captived.

BESS.

                    We much pity you.
What loss have you sustained, this Spanish prey
Shall make good to you, to the utmost farthing.

MERCHANT.

Our lives, and all our fortunes whatsoever,
Are wholly at your service.

BESS.

These gentlemen have been dejected long.
So drink our health. And pray forget not, sirs,
To pray for – (*She sees Spencer.*) Hold! Support me or I faint.

ROUGHMAN.

What sudden, unexpected ecstasy
Disturbs your conquest?

BESS.
But he was slain;
Lay buried in yon church; and thence removed,
Denied all Christian rites, and, like an infidel,
Confined unto the fields; and thence digged up,
His body, after death, had martyrdom.
All these assure me 'tis his shadow haunts me.

ROUGHMAN.
Fawcett, convey the owner to his cabin.

Exit Fawcett with Bess.

SPENCER.
I pray, sir, what young gentleman is that?

ROUGHMAN.
He's both the owner of the ship and goods,
That for some reasons hath his name concealed.

SPENCER.
I have seen a face, ere now, like that young gentleman, but not
remember where.

ROUGHMAN.
Come, gentlemen, first make your losses good,
Out of this Spanish prize. Let's then divide both several ways,
and heavens be our guide.

MERCHANT.
We towards Mamorah.

ROUGHMAN.
We where the Fates do please,
'Till we have tracked a wilderness of seas.

Flourish. Exit Merchant.

CHORUS.
Our stage so lamely can express a sea,
That we were forced by Chorus to discourse
What should have been in action. Now, imagine,
Her passion o'er, and Goodlack well recovered;
Who, had he not been wounded, and seen Spencer,
Had sure descried him. Much prize they have ta'en:
The French and Dutch she spares; only makes spoil
Of the rich Spaniard and the barbarous Turk.
And now her fame grows great in all these seas.

Music.

BESS.
Pray for English Bess.

Battle.

Pray for English Bess.

Battle.

Pray for English Bess.

CHORUS.
Imagine Bess and Goodlack under sail
Lieutenant Roughman and their ship-boy, Clem.
The seas are calm, the night is dark and still,
And Bess thinks on her Spencer lost forever.
But many miles from home she calls his name
Although she knows that he can never hear.

Then Goodlack, still much weakened by his wound,
Proposes they should set a course for England.
Bess disagrees and Roughman sides with her.
Attend and overhear their conference now.

GOODLACK.
I say the men are spent and past endurance,
The sickness to be home afflicts them all.

BESS.
But Captain, they delight as well in victories
For Queen, for country and to 'venge our foe.

ROUGHMAN.
Besides the spoils that every man will share
When every man returns with us to Foy.

CLEM.
I too prefer to voyage near and far
I am called unto the sea and not the bar.

CHORUS.
Disputing thus and thus quite lost in talk
They scarcely note the seas begin to foam,
Enraged and chaffed by whirlwinds from the south.
The billows swell, the winds grow high and loud,
The skies throw down a very waterfall
And all too late they seek for harbour where
The *Negro* may take shelter from the danger.
Now Goodlack, like a noble captain should
Commands Bess to her cabin for her safety.
No sooner she below, a mighty surge
Casts Goodlack overboard; Clem shouts above
Man lost, man lost, and Roughman must be stayed
From plunging in to save his friend from death.
One instant born aloft they touch the moon
The next the billows suck them roaring down
Until at last in sight of shore they strike
Upon a rock submerged deep beneath the main.

And split into a thousand pieces. Stay and hear
How many live, how many too are lost
And living, what the dangers, what the cost.

Scene Fourteen

Enter Bess, Roughman and Clem.

BESS.
  All is lost!

ROUGHMAN.
  Save these ourselves.

CLEM.
  For my part, I have not so much left as a clean shirt.

BESS.
  This day the mistress of many thousands,
  And a beggar now, not worth the clothes I wear.

ROUGHMAN.
  At the lowest ebb
  The tides still flow; besides, being on the ground,
  Lower we cannot fall.

BESS.
  Yes; into the ground, the grave.
  Roughman, would I were there; till then I never
  Shall have true rest. I fain would know
  What greater misery heaven can inflict,
  I have not yet endur'd:
  If there be such, I dare it; let it come.

Enter Captain of Banditties and Others.

BANDIT.
  Seize and surprise the prisoners! Thou art mine.

ROUGHMAN.
  Villain, hands off! Know'st thou whom thou offendest?

BANDIT.
  Bind her fast, and after captive him.

ROUGHMAN.
  I will rather die,
  Than suffer her sustain least injury.

Roughman is beaten off.

                                        Exit Clem.

BESS.
  What's thy purpose?

BANDIT.
  In all my travels and my quest of blood,
  I ne'er encounter'd such a beauteous prize.
  Heavens! If I thought you would accept his thanks,
  That trades in deeds of hell, I would acknowledge
  Myself in debt to you.

BESS.
  What's thy intent,
  Bold villain, that thou mak'st this preparation?

BANDIT.
  I intend to ravish thee.

BESS.
  What! Rape intended?
  I had not thought there had been such a mischief
  Devis'd for wretched woman. Ravish me!
  'Tis beyond shipwreck, poverty, or death:
  It is a word invented first in hell,
  And by the devils first spew'd upon earth:
  Man could not have invented to have given
  Such letters sound.

BANDIT.
  I trifle hours too long;
  And now to my black purpose. – Envious day,
  Gaze with thy open eyes on this night's work,
  For thus the prologue to my lust begins.

BESS.
  Help! Murder! Rape! Murder!

BANDIT.
  I'll stop your mouth from bawling.

Enter Joffer and two Guards.

JOFFER.
  Hold thy desperate fury, and arm thyself
  For my encounter.

BANDIT.
                      Hell! prevented?

                          Exit Bandit with Followers.

JOFFER.
  Unbind that beauteous lady, and pursue
  The ruffian.
  He should be captain of those bloody thieves

That haunt our mountains, and against our King
Hath oft made outrage. He that can bring his head,
Shall have a thousand crowns for his reward.

GUARD.
Go, see this proclaim'd.

BESS.
From my knees I fall flat on my face,
In bound obeisance.

JOFFER.
Rise:
That earth's too base for such pure lips to kiss.
They should rather join with a prince's, as at first
Made for such use: nay, we will have it so.
But to behold this creature, were a project
Worthy a theatre of emperors,
Nay, gods themselves, to be spectators.
I must conduct you to the city straight,
There to present you to the royal gaze
Of our great ruler, mighty King of Fez.

Exeunt omnes.

Enter Clem.

CLEM.
What shall I do? I have left my mistress; where shall I have my wages? She's peppered by this. She 'scaped drowning, which is the way of all fish, and by this is gone the way of all flesh. My lieutenant, he's sure cut to pieces among the banditties; and so had I been, had not my baker's legs stept a little aside. My noble captain is either drowned i' th' tempest, or murdered by pirates; and none is left alive but I, Clem, poor Clem! but, poor Clem, how wilt thou do now?
Now I bethink me, I have a trade; and that, they say, will stick by a man when his friends fail him. The city is hard by, and I'll see and I can be entertained to my old trade of drawing wine: if't be but an under-skinker, I care not: better do so, than, like a prodigal, feed upon husks and acorns. Well, if I chance to lead my life under some happy sign,
To my countrymen still I'll fill the best wine.

Exit Clem.

Enter Roughman, bleeding.

ROUGHMAN.
Wounded, but 'scap'd with life: but Bess's loss; that's it that grieves me inward. Ravished, perhaps, and murdered. Oh, if Goodlack survive, how would he blame my cowardice! A thread spun may be untwined, but things in nature done, undone can never be. She's lost, and I surviving, left to the earth most miserable. No means to raise myself? I met a pursuivant, even now, proclaiming to the man who could bring the head of the banditties' captain, for his reward a thousand crowns: if not for gain of gold, yet for he injured Bess, that shall be my next task. What, though I die,
Be this my comfort, that it chanc'd me well,
To perish by his hand by whom she fell.

Exit Roughman.

Scene Fifteen

Morocco. The court.
Enter Mullisheg and Bashaw Alcade with other Attendants.

MULLISHEG.
Out of these bloody and intestine broils
We have at length attained a fortunate peace,
And now at last established in the throne
Of our great ancestors, and reign as King
Of Fez and great Morocco.

ALCADE.
Mighty Mullisheg,
Pride of our age and glory of the Moors,
By whose victorious hand all Barbary
Is conquered, awed and swayed, behold thy vassals
With loud applauses greet thy victory.

Shout. Flourish.

MULLISHEG.
Upon the slaughtered bodies of our foes
We mount our high tribunal: and being sole,
Without competitor, we now have leisure
To stablish laws, first for our kingdom's safety,
The enriching of our public treasury,
And last our state and pleasure; then give order
That all such christian Merchants as have traffic
And freedom in our country, that conceal
The least part of our custom due to us,
Shall forfeit ship and goods.
Those forfeitures must help to furnish up
The exhausted treasure that our wars consumed;
Part of such profits as accrue that way
We have already tasted.

ALCADE.
'Tis most fit
Those Christians that reap profit by our land

Should contribute unto so great a loss.

MULLISHEG.
Alcade, they shall. – But what's the style of king
Without his pleasure? Find us concubines,
The fairest Christian damsels you can hire,
Or buy for gold; the loveliest of the Moors
We can command and negroes everywhere:

Enter Bashaw Joffer.

Italians, French and Dutch, choice Turkish girls,
Must fill our Alkedavy, the great palace
Where Mullisheg now deigns to keep his court.

ALCADE.
Who else are worthy to be libertines but such as beat the sword?

JOFFER.
Great Mullisheg, unspeak your last commandment
And send no more to seek for concubines.

MULLISHEG.
If kings on earth be termed demigods,
Why should we not make here terrestrial heaven?
We can, we will: our God shall be our pleasure;
For so our Meccan prophet warrants us.

JOFFER.
Behold your God has heard and hearing answer'd
That Mullisheg must have his just reward.

Bess is revealed.

MULLISHEG.
Joffer, thou pleasest us.
I ne'er beheld a beauty more complete.

ALCADE.
To describe her were to make eloquence dumb.

MULLISHEG.
Thou hast inflamed our spirits. Whence is she?
Where was she found and why in disarray?

JOFFER.
Great lord, while I was hunting by the shore
I heard a piteous cry that chilled my blood.
I found this peerless beauty bound to a tree
And pleading for her almost forfeit chastity,
Which but for my unlook'd for coming in
Her ruffian captors would have soon enjoyed.

BESS.
Long live the high and mighty King of Fez!

MULLISHEG.
Where were you bred?

BESS.
                    In England, royal sir.

ALCADE.
In England?

MULLISHEG.
            By what strange adventure, then,
Happen'd she on these coasts?

JOFFER.
By shipwreck, mighty sovereign.

MULLISHEG.
                    On what coast,
Pray, were you shipwrecked?

BESS.
Upon these neighbouring shores.
I was this morning rich in wealth and servants
But yet by midday I commanded neither.
Next by the bandits was I doomed to death.
Not death alone but death with infamy.
I, that this morn commanded half a million,
Have nothing now – I cannot speak without tears.
I would my friends were safe and that the sea
Had swallowed me and me alone.

MULLISHEG.
Augment your griefs no farther.
I am amazed!
This is not mortal creature I behold,
But some bright angel, that is dropped from heaven,
Sent by our prophet.

ALCADE.
A woman born in England?

MULLISHEG.
That English earth may well be termed a heaven.
That breeds such divine beauties. Make me sure
That thou art mortal by one friendly touch.

BESS.
Keep off.

MULLISHEG.
            Now, by the prophet we adore:
You shall live lady of your free desires:
'Tis love, not force, must quench our amorous fires.
Say, in England, what's your fashion and garb of entertainment?

BESS.
    Our first greeting
Begins still on the lips.

MULLISHEG.
    Fair creature, shall I be immortalized
With that high favour?

BESS.
                        'Tis no immodest thing
You ask, nor shame for Bess to kiss a king.

She kisses him.

MULLISHEG.
    This kiss hath all my vitals ecstasied.
Grace me so much as take you seat by me.

BESS.
    I'll be so far commanded.

MULLISHEG.
    Sweet, your age?

BESS.
                    Not fully yet seventeen.

MULLISHEG.
    But how your birth?
And what your cause to travel?

BESS.
                        Mighty prince,
If you desire to see me beat my breast,
Pour forth a river of increasing tears,
Then you may urge me to that sad discourse.

MULLISHEG.
    Not for Mamorah's wealth, nor all the gold
Coined in rich Barbary. Nay, sweet, arise,
And ask of me, be't half this kingdom's treasure,
And thou art lady on't.

BESS.
    If I shall ask, 't must be, you will not give.
Our country breeds no beggars; for our hearts
Are of more noble temper.

MULLISHEG.
                        Sweet, your name?

BESS.
    Elizabeth.

MULLISHEG.
                    There's virtue in that name.
The Virgin Queen, so famous through the world,
The mighty Empress of the maiden isle,
Whose predecessors have o'er-run great France,
Whose powerful hand doth still support the Dutch,
And keeps the potent King of Spain in awe,
Is not she titled so?

BESS.
                        She is.

MULLISHEG.
    Hath she herself a face so fair as yours,
When she appears for wonder?

BESS.
                        Mighty Fez,
You cast a blush upon my maiden cheek,
To pattern me with her. Why, England's Queen,
She is the only phoenix of her age,
The pride and glory of the Western Isles.
Had I a thousand tongues, they all would tire,
And fail me in her true description.

MULLISHEG.
    Grant me this:
Tomorrow we supply our judgment seat,
And sentence causes; sit with us in state,
And let your presence beautify our throne.

BESS.
    In that I am your servant.

MULLISHEG.
                        And we thine.
We will have banquets, revels, and what not,
To entertain this stranger.
Set on in state, attendants, and full train.
But find to ask, we vow thou shalt obtain.

ALCADE.
    Bashaw, this King is mightily in love.

                                    Exeunt omnes.

Scene Sixteen

A tavern.
Enter Clem dressed as a Moor.

CLEM.

Oh! The fortune of the seas: never did man that marries a whore so cast himself away, as I had been like i' th' last tempest: yet nothing vexes me so much, that after all my travels, no man that meets me but may say, and say very truly, I am now no better than a pot companion.

Enter Goodlack.

GOODLACK.

Where were I best to lodge? First drink here, and after make enquiry who's the best host for strangers.
Come, ho! where be these drawers?

CLEM.

Gentleman, I draw none myself, but I'll send some.
Score a quart! Ha!

GOODLACK.

How!

CLEM.

No, no; I am an ass, a very animal.

GOODLACK.

Why dost thou bear the wine back?

CLEM.

It cannot be.

GOODLACK.

What! doest thou think me such a cashier'd soldier, that I have no cash?

CLEM.

Tush! it cannot be he.

GOODLACK.

Set down the wine.

CLEM.

I will, I will, sir. – Score a quart of – tricks, mere phantasms. Shall I draw wine to shadows? So, I might add up th' score and find no substance to pay for it.

GOODLACK.

Sirrah, set down the wine.

CLEM.

Some Italian mountebanks: upon my life, mere juggling.

GOODLACK.

Upon my life 'tis Clem.

CLEM.

Ca – Ca – Capt – Captain! Master Goodlack!

GOODLACK.

Clem?

CLEM.

I am Clem.

GOODLACK.

And I Goodlack, but cannot think thee Clem.

CLEM.

Yes, I am Clem, of Foy, turned a bashaw of Barbary.

GOODLACK.

Oh, tell me and be brief in thy relation
What happen'd you after the sudden tempest.
What's become of Bess? Where did the *Negro* touch?

CLEM.

I'll give you a touch, take it as you will. – The *Negro*, and all that was in her, was wrecked on the coast of Barbary; she, and all the wealth that was in her, all drowned i' the' bottom of the sea.

GOODLACK.

No matter for the riches; where's she, worth more than ship or goods?

CLEM.

She, Roughman, and I, were all cast ashore safe, like so many drowned rats; where we were no sooner landed, but were set upon by the banditties, where she was bound to a tree, and ready to be ravished by the captain of the outlaws.

GOODLACK.

Oh! Worse than shipwreck could be.

CLEM.

I see Roughman half cut in pieces with rescuing her; but whether the other half be alive, or no, I cannot tell. For my own part, I made shift for one, my heels doing me better service than my hands; and coming to the city, having no other means to live by, got me to my old trade to draw wine.

GOODLACK.

Ravished? And Roughman slain?

CLEM.

Comfort, sir, and tell me rather how you came ashore.

GOODLACK.

What is this world? What's man? Are we created
Out of flint, or iron, that we are made to bear this?

CLEM.

Your only way is to drink wine, if you be in grief; for that's the only way, the old proverb says, to comfort the heart.

GOODLACK.

Here will I lie; and I prithee, Clem, let's hear from thee; but now I'll leave thee.

Exit Goodlack.

CLEM.

Let me see – three quarts, two pottles, one gallon, and a pint; one pint, two quarts more, then I have my load: thus are we that are under-journeymen put to't.

Enter Joffer, Alcade, Bess and Attendants.

JOFFER.

Will you walk, lady.

BESS.

That we the streets more freely may survey,
We'll walk along.
That should be Clem, my man. – Give me some gold. –
Here, sirrah; drink to the health
Of thy old mistress. – Usher on:
We have more serious things to think upon.

Exeunt.

CLEM.

Mistress Bess! Mistress Elizabeth! 'tis she. Hah! Gold! Hence, pewter pots; I'll be a pewter porter no longer. My mistress turned gallant; and shall I do nothing but run upstairs and downstairs with 'Anon, anon, sir'? No; I'll send these pots home by some porter or other, put myself into a better habit, and say, the case is altered: then will I go home to the Bush, where I drew wine, and buy out my time, and take up my chamber; be served in pomp by my fellow prentices.

Re-enter Goodlack.

GOODLACK.

How now, Clem! you loiter here? the house is full of guests, and you are extremely called for.

CLEM.

You are deceived, my Captain, I'll assure you: you speak to as good a man as myself. Do you want any money?

GOODLACK.

Canst thou lend me any?

CLEM.

Look; I am the lord of these mines, of these Indies.

GOODLACK.

How camest thou by them?

CLEM.

A delicate, sweet lady, meeting me i' th' street, and being enamoured of my good parts, gave me this gold. But if you want any money, speak in time; for, if I once turn courtier I will scorn my poor friends, look scurvily upon my acquaintance, borrow of all men, be beholding to any man; and my motto shall be, Base is the man that pays.

GOODLACK.

But, Clem, how camest thou by this gold?

CLEM.

News, news! Though not the lost sheep, yet the lost shrew is found – my mistress, Mistress Elizabeth, 'tis she. She, meeting me i' th' street, seeing I had a pot or two too much, gave me ten pounds in a purse to pay for it: *Ecce Signum*. 'Tis she, 'tis she, 'tis she.

Re-enter Bess, Joffer, Alcade, Attendants.

JOFFER.

Way there for the King's mistress.

GOODLACK.

Hah! The King's mistress, said he?

BESS.

Keep off, we would have no such rubs as these
Trouble our way, but have them swept aside.

ALCADE.

Give back, you trouble the presence!

Bess casts a jewel.

BESS.

A company of base companions.

GOODLACK.

This cannot be Bess, but some fury hath stolen her shape.

CLEM.

Observ'd you not this jewel she cast to you.
See, see the paper which it wrap't should tell us more.

GOODLACK.

Follow to the palace. Show this ring.
Tell all who ask, you are of the English train.
Come, Clem, and leave your pewter and your pots
We must obey or spoil our mistress' plots.

CLEM.

I follow, Captain, let us presently thither,
Where I will flourish it in my cap and feather.

Scene Seventeen

The palace.
Enter Spencer.

SPENCER.

    This day the King ascends his royal throne.
    The honest merchant, in whose ship I came,
    Hath, by a cunning quiddit in the law,
    Both ship and goods made forfeit to the King,
    To whom I will petition. But no more;
    He's now upon his entrance.

Hautboys.

Enter Alcade and Joffer at one door, Clem at the other.

ALCADE.

    Sir, by your leave, you're of the English train?

CLEM.

    I am so, thou great monarch of the Mauritanians.

JOFFER.

    Then, 'tis the King's command we give you all attendance.

CLEM.

    Great Signior of the Saracens, I thank thee.

ALCADE.

    Will you walk in to the chamber?

CLEM.

    I will make bold to march in towards your chamber.

Enter Two Merchants.

1ST MERCHANT.

    I pray, sir, are you of the English train?

CLEM.

    Why, what art thou, my friend?

1ST MERCHANT.

    Sir, a French merchant, run into relapse,
    And forfeit of the law. Here's for you, sir,
    Forty good Barbary pieces, to deliver
    Your lady this petition, who, I hear,
    Can all things with the King.

CLEM.

    Your gold doth bind me to you – I no sooner put my nose into
    the court, but my hand itches for a bribe already. – What's your
    business, my friend?

2ND MERCHANT.

    Some of my men, for a little outrage done,
    Are sentenced to the galleys.

CLEM.

    To the gallows?

2ND MERCHANT.

    No; to the galleys. Now, could your lady purchase
    Their pardon from the King, there's twenty angels.

CLEM.

    What are you, sir?

2ND MERCHANT.

    A Florentine merchant.

CLEM.

    Then you are, as they say, a Christian?

2ND MERCHANT.

    Heaven forbid, else!

CLEM.

    I should not have the faith to take your gold, else.
    Attend on me: I'll speak in your behalf.
    Where be my bashaws? Usher us in state:
    And when we sit to banquet, see you wait.

Flourish..

Enter Mullisheg and Bess with all the other train.

MULLISHEG.

    Here seat thee, maid of England, like a queen
    The style we'll give thee, wilt though deign us love.

BESS.

    May it please you, high and mighty Mullisheg,
    The captain of my ship so lately lost
    Who I confess, I fear'd was lost as well,
    Now craves admittance to your Highness presence.

MULLISHEG.

    Give him the entertainment of a Prince.

GOODLACK.

    Long live the high and mighty King of Fez.

MULLISHEG (*to Bess*).

    Hark what I proffer thee. Continue here
    And grant me full fruition of thy love.

ALCADE.

    Bring forth the prisoners and petitioners.

BESS.

Good.

MULLISHEG.

Thou shalt have all my peers to honour thee,
Next our great prophet.

BESS.

Well.

MULLISHEG.

And when thou'rt weary of our sun-burnt clime,
Thy vessel shall be ballast home with gold.

Bess sees Spencer with the prisoners.

BESS.

Bless me, you holy angels!

MULLISHEG.

What is't offends you, sweet?

SPENCER.

I am amazed, and know not what to think on't.

BESS.

Captain, dost not see? Is not that Spencer's ghost?

GOODLACK.

I see and, like you, am ecstasied.

SPENCER.

If mine eyes mistake not,
That should be Captain Goodlack, and that Bess.
But oh! I cannot be so happy.

GOODLACK.

'Tis he, and I'll salute him.

BESS.

Captain, stay. You shall be swayed by me.

SPENCER.

Him I well know; but how should she come hither?

MULLISHEG.

What is't that troubles you?

BESS.

                Most mighty King,
Spare me no longer time but to bestow
My captain on a message.

MULLISHEG.

Thou shalt command my silence, and his ear.

BESS

(to Goodlack). Go wind about, and when you see least eyes
Are fixed on you, single him out, and see
If we mistake not. If he be the man,
Give me some private note.

GOODLACK.

This. *(Making a sign.)*

BESS.

Enough. – What said your highness?

MULLISHEG.

You mind me not, sweet virgin.

BESS.

You talk of love:
My lord, I'll tell you more of that hereafter;
But now to your state-business.

JOFFER.

                  The King speaks.

MULLISHEG.

Our laws are firm, our will implacable.
All Christian merchants freely traffic here
But should they to avoid the custom due
Conceal the least part which is owed to us
Their ships and goods are forfeit to our throne
And without our mercy, forfeit life as well.

Goodlack makes a sign.

BESS.

Now, all you sad disasters, dare your worst;
I neither care nor fear: my Spencer lives!

The Prisoners are brought forward.

1ST MERCHANT.

Pray, sir, remember me.

2ND MERCHANT.

                Good sir, my suit.

CLEM.

I am perfect in both your parts, without prompting. Mistress,
here are two Christen friends of mine have forfeited ships and
men, one word from your lips might get their release. I have
had a feeling of the business already.

MULLISHEG.

For dealing in commodities forbid,
You're fined a thousand ducats.

BESS.
Cast off the burden of your heavy doom.
A follower of my train petitions for him.

MULLISHEG.
One of thy train, sweet Bess?
Well, sirrah, for your lady's sake
His ship and goods shall be restored again.

3RD MERCHANT.
Long live the King of Fez!

CLEM.
Mistress, another friend; ay, and paid beforehand.

MULLISHEG.
Sirrah, your men, for outrage and contempt,
Are doomed to the galleys.

BESS.
A censure too severe for Christians.

MULLISHEG.
Thy word shall be their ransom: they're discharged.
What grave old man is that?

JOFFER.
A Christian preacher; one that would convert your Moors, and
turn them to a new belief.

MULLISHEG.
Then he shall die, as we are King of Fez.

BESS.
For these I only spake; for him I kneel,
If I have any grace with mighty Fez.

MULLISHEG.
We can deny thee nothing, beauteous maid.
A kiss shall be his pardon.

BESS.
                            Thus I pay't.

CLEM.
Must your black face be smouching my mistress' white lips! I
would you had kissed her a –

ALCADE.
Hah! how is that, sir?

CLEM.
I know what I say, sir; I would he had kissed her a –

ALCADE.
A – what?

CLEM.
A thousand times, to have done him a pleasure!

SPENCER.
'Sfoot! I could tear my hair off.
Hold me Goodlack, or I shall break out
Into some dangerous outrage.

GOODLACK.
Show in this your wisdom, and quite suppress your fury.

MULLISHEG.
That kiss was worth the ransom of a king.

SPENCER.
To make you more renowned, great king, and us the more
indebted, there's an Englishman
Hath forfeited his ship for goods uncustomed. –
I pray set ship and goods and merchant free.

MULLISHEG (*to Bess*).
If you would find me merciful once more
Second your kindness: let these bashaws see
Your tempting lips solely belong to me.

SPENCER.
This is beyond all durance, all restraint.
To thee alone? Insulting, bragging Moor!

A brawl. Spencer is subdued.

MULLISHEG.
What's he, of that brave presence?

BESS.
A gentleman of England,
Do him some grace, for my sake.

MULLISHEG.
For thy sake what would not I perform?
He shall have grace and honour.

He goes to Joffer.

Joffer, go see him prepared to attend on us:
He shall be our chief eunuch.

They seize Spencer. Coming down to them.

BESS.
Not for ten worlds. Whate'er he be, I beg
That I may be his sentencer.

MULLISHEG.
                            Thou shalt.

BESS.
Let me descend; and ere I judge the felon,
Survey him first. 'Tis pity; for it seems
He hath an honest face. –
Good outward parts; but in a foreign clime,
Shame your own country? –
An indifferent proper man, and take these courses?

SPENCER.
I fear my heart will break,
It doth so struggle for irruption forth.

MULLISHEG.
When do you speak his sentence, lady?

BESS.
You'll confirm 't, whate'er it be?

MULLISHEG.
As we are king, we will.

BESS.
Set forth the prisoner.

JOFFER.
Stand forward, Englishman.

BESS.
Then hear thy doom. Thy friend and thou art free.
Thy life's my gift. I give myself to thee.

MULLISHEG.
Lady, we understand not this.

BESS.
And have I found my Spencer.

CLEM.
Please your majesty, I see all men are not capable of honour:
what he refuseth, may it please you to bestow on me.

MULLISHEG.
With all my heart. Go bear him hence, Alcade.
Into our Alkedavy: honour him.
And let him taste the razor.

CLEM.
                    There's honour for me!

ALCADE.
Come, follow.

CLEM.
No, sir; I'll go before you, for mine honour.

                    Exeunt Clem and Alcade.

SPENCER.
Oh! show yourself, renowned King, the same
Fame blazons you. Bestow this maid on me:
'Tis such a gift as kingdoms cannot buy.
She is a precedent to all true love,
And shall be registered to aftertimes,
That ne'er shall pattern her.

GOODLACK.
Heard you the story of their constant love,
'Twould move in you compassion.

MULLISHEG.
You have wakened in me an heroic spirit:
Lust shall not conquer virtue. – Till this hour,
We graced thee for thy beauty, English woman;
But now we wonder at thy constancy.

BESS.
Oh! Were you of our faith, I'd swear great Mullisheg
To be a god on earth. – and lives my Spencer?
In troth I thought thee dead.

SPENCER.
In hope of thee,
I lived to gain both life and liberty.

Enter Roughman.

ROUGHMAN.
Can any man show me the great King of Fez?

JOFFER.
Behold the King.

ROUGHMAN.
Deign then, renowned King, to cast thy eyes
Upon a poor dejected gentleman,
Whom fortune hath dejected even to nothing.
I have nor meat nor money: these rags are all my riches.
Only necessity compels me claim
A debt owing by you.

MULLISHEG.
                    By us?
Let's know the sum, and how the debt accrues.

ROUGHMAN.
You have proclaim'd to him could bring the head
Of the banditties' captain, for his reward,
A thousand crowns. Now, I being a gentleman,
A traveller, and in want, made this my way
To raise my ruin'd hope. I singled him,

Fought with him hand to hand, and from his bloody shoulders
Lopped his head.

MULLISHEG.

Boldy and bravely done. Whate'er thou be,
Thou shalt receive it from our treasury.
From what country do you claim your birth?

ROUGHMAN.

From England, royal sir.

MULLISHEG.

            These bold Englishmen,
I think, are all compos'd of spirit and fire;
The element of earth hath no part in them.

BESS.

Is there a braver man alive? What think you?

ROUGHMAN.

Let me no longer live in ecstasy;
This wonder will confound me. – Noble friends,
Bootless it were to ask you why, because
I find you here. – Illustrious King, you owe
Me nothing now; to show me these, is reward
Beyond what you proclaim'd: the rest I'll pardon.

MULLISHEG

(to Spencer). All your strange fortunes we will hear discoursed,
And after that your fair espousals grace,
If you can find a man of your belief
To do that grateful office.

SPENCER.

            None more fit
Than this religious and brave gentlemen,
Late rescued from death's sentence.

PREACHER.

None more proud.
To do you that poor service.

ROUGHMAN.

Oh! that we three so happily should meet,
And want the fourth.

Re-enter Clem, running.

CLEM.

No more of your honour, sir, if you love me! Is this your
Moorish preferment, to rob a man of his best jewels?

MULLISHEG.

Hast thou seen our Alkedavy?

CLEM.

Davy do you call him? He may be called shavy;
No more of your cutting honour, if you love me. Roughman!

ROUGHMAN.

But what adventure hath preferr'd you,
And brought you thus in grace?

GOODLACK.

            You shall hereafter
Partake of that at large.

MULLISHEG.

Come, beauteous maid; we'll see thee crowned a bride.
At all our pompous banquets these shall wait
Thy followers and thy servants press with gold;
And not the mean'st that to thy train belongs,
But shall approve our bounty. Lead in state,
And, wheresoe'er thy fame shall be enrolled,
The world report thou art a Girl worth gold.

Exeunt omnes.

Scene Eighteen

The palace.
Enter Tota, Mullisheg's wife.

TOTA.

It must not, may not, shall not endur'd.
Left we for this our country, to be made
A mere neglected lady here in Fez?
Can womanish ambition, heat of blood,
Or height of birth, brook this, and not revenge?
Revenge? On whom? On mighty Mullisheg?
We are not safe then. On the English stranger?
And why on her, when there's no apprehension
That can in thought pollute her innocence?
Yet something I must do. What! Nothing yet?

Enter Bashaw Joffer.

JOFFER.

Call'd Your Majesty?

TOTA.

No; yet I think I did. Begone: yet stay. –
Will not this misshapen embryo grow to form?
Not yet? Nor yet?

JOFFER.

            I attend Your Highness' pleasure.

TOTA.
'Tis perfect, and I ha'it.

JOFFER.
I wait still.

TOTA.
The King no way in peril; she secure;
None harm'd; all pleas'd; I sweetly satisfied,
And yet reveng'd at full.

JOFFER.
You need not me.

TOTA.
Say, where's the King?

JOFFER.
I' the presence.

TOTA.
How?

JOFFER.
Distemper'd, late, and strangely humorous,
The cause none can conjecture.

TOTA.
Is the King upon his entrance?

JOFFER.
'Tis thought he is.
If so, this strange sudden distemperature
Hath not his purpose alter'd.

TOTA.
You have leave
To leave us, and attend the King.

JOFFER.
I shall.

TOTA.
If any of the English lady's train
Come in your way, you may request them hither.
Say, I would question some things of their country.

JOFFER.
Madam, I shall.

Enter Clem, meeting Joffer.

JOFFER.
'Tis the Queen's pleasure you attend her.

CLEM.
The Queen speak with me? Can you tell the business?

JOFFER.
Yonder she walks. I leave you.

Exit Joffer.

TOTA.
Now, sir; you are of England?

CLEM.
And I think you are a witch.

TOTA.
How, sirrah?

CLEM.
A foolish proverb we use in our country; which, to give you in other words, is as much as to say, you have hit the nail on the head.

TOTA.
You have seen both nations, England and our Fez: how do our people differ?

CLEM.
Our countrymen eat and drink as yours do; open their eyes, when they would see, and shut them again, when they would sleep: gape when their mouths open, as yours: and scratch when it itcheth.

TOTA.
Canst thou be secret to me, Englishman?

CLEM.
Yes, and chaste, too: I have ta'en a medicine for't.

TOTA.
Be fix'd to me in what I shall employ thee,
Constant and private unto my designs,
More grace and honour I will do to thee
Than e'er thou didst receive from Mullisheg.

CLEM.
Grace and honour! His grace and honour was to take away some part, and she would honour me to take away all, I'll see you damned, first!

TOTA.
Mistake me not.

CLEM.
Grace and honour, quotha!

TOTA.
Sure, this fellow is some sot.

Enter Roughamn.

ROUGHMAN.
How now, Clem; wither in such post-haste?

CLEM.
There, if you will have any grace and honour, you may pay for't
as dear as I have done. 'Sfoot! I have little enough left: I would
fain carry away something into my own country.

TOTA.
This should have better sense. I'll next prove him.

ROUGHMAN.
Excuse me, mighty princess, that my boldness
Hath press'd thus far into your privacies.

TOTA.
You no way have offended. Nay, come near:
We love to grace a stranger. I have observ'd you
To be of some command amongst the English;
Nor make I question but that you may be
Of fair revenues.

ROUGHMAN.
                    A poor gentleman.

TOTA.
We'll make thee rich. Spend that.

ROUGHMAN.
                              Your grace's bounty
Exceeds what merit can make good in me.
I am Your Highness' servant.

TOTA.
Let that jewel be worn as our high favour.

ROUGHMAN.
'Sfoot! I think
This Queen's in love with me. – Madam, I shall.

TOTA.
If any favour I can do in court
Can make you farther gracious, speak it freely:
What power we have is yours.

ROUGHMAN.
Doubtless it is so, and I am made for ever.

TOTA.
Nay, we shall take it ill to give ourselves

So amply to your knowledge, and you not use us.

ROUGHMAN.
Use us! Now, upon my life, she's caught
What! Courted by a queen – a royal princess?
Where were your eyes, Bess, that you could not see
These hidden parts and mysteries which this Queen
Hath in my shape observ'd? 'Tis but a fortune
That I was born to; and I thank heaven for't.

TOTA.
May I trust you?

ROUGHMAN.
                    With your life, with your honour.
I'll be as private to you as your heart
Within your bosom.

TOTA.
I'll prove so.

ROUGHMAN.
Madam, let this –

TOTA.
What?

ROUGHMAN.
This kiss.

TOTA.
This fool! This ass! This insolent gull!

ROUGHMAN.
Why, did not your grace mean plainly?

TOTA.
In what, sir?

ROUGHMAN.
Did you not court me?

TOTA.
How! That face?
Think'st thou I could love a monkey – a baboon?
Know, were I mounted in the height of lust,
And a mere prostitute, rather than thee
I'd embrace one – name but that creature
That thou dost think most odious.

ROUGHMAN.
Pardon me, lady:
I humbly take my leave.

TOTA.
Yet you are not gone.
Know, then, you have incurr'd
The King's wrath first, our high displeasure next,
The least of which is death. Yet, will you grow
More near unto my present purposes,
I will not only pardon you what's past,
but multiply my bounties.

ROUGHMAN.
I am your prisoner.

TOTA.
And yet a free man. I am injured highly,
And thou must aid me in my just revenge.

ROUGHMAN.
Were it to combat the most valiant Moor
That ever Fez, Morocco, or Argiers bred,
I for your sake would do it.

TOTA.
We seek not blood,
Nor to expose thee to the least of danger.
I am modest; and what I dare not trust my own tongue with,
Or thoughts, I'll boldy give unto thine ears.
List – Do you shake your head?

ROUGHMAN.
Wrong my friend?

TOTA.
Is not our life,
Our honour, all in your hand, and will you lavish us,
Or scant that bounty should crown you with excess?

ROUGHMAN.
I'll pause upon't.

TOTA.
Is not your life ours, by your insolence?
Have we not power to take it?

ROUGHMAN.
Say no more: I'll do it.

TOTA.
But may I hope?

ROUGHMAN.
I have cast all doubts, and know how it may be compass'd.

TOTA.
Take the advantage of this night.

ROUGHMAN.
Expect fair end.
All doubts are cast.

TOTA.
So make a queen thy friend.

Recorders.

Enter Mullisheg, Joffer, and Alcade, Goodlack, Bess, and the rest.

MULLISHEG.
All music's harsh: command these discords cease;
For we have war within us.

BESS.
Mighty King,
What is't offends Your Highness?

MULLISHEG.
Nothing, Bess.
Yet all things do. – Oh, what did I bestow,
When I gave her away!

BESS.
The Queen attends you.

MULLISHEG.
Let her attend.

TOTA.
Ay, King. – Neglected still,
My just revenge shall wound, although not kill.

MULLISHEG.
I was a traitor to my own desires,
To part with her so slightly. What! No means
To alter these proceedings?

SPENCER.
Strange disturbances.

GOODLACK.
What might the project be?

MULLISHEG.
And Fez, why a king, and not command thy pleasure?
Is she not within our kingdom? Nay within our palace?
And therefore in our power. Is she alone
That happiness that I desire on earth?
Which, since the heavens have given up to mine hands,
Shall I despise their bounty – and not rather
Run through a thousand dangers, to enjoy
Their prodigal favours? Dangers! Tush! there's none.

We are here amidst our people, wall'd with subjects round,
And danger is our slave: besides, our war
Is with weak woman. Oh! But I have sworn
And seal'd to her safe conduct. What of that?
Can a king swear against his own desires,
I should commit high treason 'gainst myself,
Not to do that might give my soul content,
And satisfy my appetite with fulness. –
Alcade!

ALCADE.
My Lord.

MULLISHEG.
Rides the English Merchant still within the harbour?

ALCADE.
Some league from land.

MULLISHEG.
Lest that these English should attempt escape,
Now they are laden fully with our bounties,
Cast thou a watchful eye upon these two.

ALCADE.
I shall.

MULLISHEG.
How goes the hour?

ALCADE.
About some four.

MULLISHEG.
We rose too soon, Bess, from your nuptial feasts:
Something we tasted made us stomach sick,
But now we find a more contentful change.

BESS.
Your sunshine is our day.

MULLISHEG.
Dispose yourselves
All to your free desires; pleasure shall spring
From us to flow on you.

ALL.
Long live the King!

MULLISHEG.
To your free pastimes: leave us.

Exeunt. Manent Goodlack and Mullisheg.

MULLISHEG.
Captain, stay. Captain, I read a fortune in thy brow.

GOODLACK.
That I can do?

MULLISHEG.
It lies in thee to raise thy ruin'd fortunes
As high as is a viceroy's,
And to command, in all our territories.

GOODLACK.
Golden promises.

MULLISHEG.
We do not feed with air: it lies in thee.
We two may grapple souls, be friends and brothers.

GOODLACK.
Teach me how.

MULLISHEG.
I do not find thee coming: in thy looks
I cannot spy that fresh alacrity,
Should meet our love half-way.

GOODLACK.
You wonder me.

MULLISHEG.
No; thou art dull, or fearful. Fare thee well.

GOODLACK.
Forspeak me not. I am of no shrinking temper.

MULLISHEG.
I am drowsy on the sudden: whilst I sleep,
Captain, read there.

He counterfeits sleep, and gives him a letter.

GOODLACK.
'*To make Bess mine, some secret means devise,
To thy own height and heart I'll make thee rise*'. –
Is not thin ink the blood of basilisks,
That kills me in the eyes, and blinds me so,
That I can read no further? Oh, my fate!
Nothing but this? This? Had a parliament
Of fiends and furies in a synod sat,
And devis'd, plotted, parley'd and contriv'd,
They scarce could second this. What does my face
Prognosticate, that he should find writ there
An index of such treasons? Not to do it,
May purchase his displeasure, which can be

No less than death, or bondage, but what more?
'We are impatient of delays; this night
Let it be done.'

Mullisheg starts out of his chair, as from a dream.

MULLISHEG.
If he fail,
I'll have his flesh cut small as winter's snow,
Or summer's atoms.

GOODLACK.
                        Ha! Was that by us?

MULLISHEG.
Where was I? – Oh! I dreamed upon the sudden:
How fast was I.

GOODLACK.
                        A fair warning 'twas. –

MULLISHEG.
Who's i' th' next room?

GOODLACK.
                        My lord.

MULLISHEG.
My Captain, was it thou?
Did you read
That scroll we gave you, Captain?

GOODLACK.
Add to your work a business of more danger
That I may think me worthy.

MULLISHEG.
                        Think'st thou, Captain,
It may be easily compass'd?

GOODLACK.
                        Dare you trust me?

MULLISHEG.
I dare.

GOODLACK.
        Then know, besides to dare and can, I will.
I'll set my brains in action.

MULLISHEG.
                        Noble friend,
Above thy thoughts our honours shall extend.

GOODLACK.
I am not to be shaken.

MULLISHEG.
Where be our eunuchs? We will have
Rare change of music shrill and high,
That shall exceed the spheres in harmony.
The jewels of her habit shall reflect,
To daze all eyes that shall behold her state.
In wild moriscos we will lead the bride;
Our treasure shall like to a torrent rush
Streams of rewards, richer than Tagus' sands,
To make these English strangers swim in gold.
Make this night mine, as we are King of Fez,
Th'art Viceroy, Captain.

Exit Mullisheg.

GOODLACK.
Oh, my brain,
In what a labyrinth art thou! Solicit her,
In treason towards my friend?

Enter Roughman.

ROUGHMAN.
I am to solicit Spencer
To lie with the Moor's queen; a business Bess
Will hardly thank me for.

GOODLACK.
Impossibilities all: the more I wade,
The more I drown in weakness.

ROUGHMAN.
Captain.

GOODLACK.
Oh! Lieutenant,
Never was man perplex'd thus.

ROUGHMAN.
What! As you?
Captain, a whole school of sophisters
Could not unriddle me.

GOODLACK.
Tell me thy grievances, and unto thee
I will unveil my bosom: both disclos'd
I'll beg in mine thy counsel and assistance:
Thy cause shall mine command.

ROUGHMAN.
A heart, a hand.

GOODLACK.
I am to woo fair Bess to lie with Mullisheg.

ROUGHMAN.
And I woo Spencer to embrace the Queen.

GOODLACK.
Is't possible?

ROUGHMAN.
'Tis more than possible; 'tis absolutely past.

GOODLACK.
There's not a hair to choose. Canst counsel me?

ROUGHMAN.
Can you advise me?

GOODLACK.
I am past my wits.

ROUGHMAN.
And I beyond all sense.

GOODLACK.
Wouldst thou do't?

ROUGHMAN.
What! For gold betray my friend and country?
Would you, Captain?

GOODLACK.
What! And wear a sword
To guard my honour and a Christian's faith?

ROUGHMAN.
Nobly resolved.

GOODLACK.
– 'Sfoot! has thou no project? Dost thou partake my dullness?

ROUGHMAN.
The more I strive, the more I am entangled.

GOODLACK.
And I, too. – Not yet?

ROUGHMAN.
Nor yet, nor ever.

GOODLACK.
'Twas coming here, and now again 'tis vanish'd.

ROUGHMAN.
Call't back again, for heaven's sake.

GOODLACK.
Again.

ROUGHMAN.
Thanks, heaven!

GOODLACK.
And now again 'tis gone.

ROUGHMAN.
Can you not catch fast hold on't?

GOODLACK.
Give me away.

Enter Spencer, Bess and Clem.

SPENCER.
The King was wondrous pleasant. – Oh! my Bess.

BESS.
Could my Spencer
Think that a barbarous Moor could be so train'd
In human virtues?

CLEM.
Fie upon't! I am so tired with dancing with these same black she chimney-sweepers and I have so tickled them with our country dances, Sillenger's Round, and Tom Tiler. We have so fiddled it!

SPENCER.
Sirrah, what will you tell your friends, when you return into England?

CLEM.
First and foremost, I have observed the wisdom of these Moors: for some two days since, being invited to one of the chief bashaws to dinner, after meat, seated by a huge fire, and feeling his shins to burn, I requested him to pull back his chair, but he very understandingly sent for three or four masons, and removed the chimney. The same Moorian entreated me to lie with him; and I, willing to have a candle burning by, but he by no means would grant it: I asked him why. 'No,' says he, 'we'll put out the light, that the fleas may not know where to find us.'

BESS.
Out with't at once, Lieutenant.

SPENCER.
Captain, speak.

GOODLACK.
W'are all lost.

ROUGHMAN.
All shipwrecked.

CLEM.
Are we ashore, and shall we be cast away?

SPENCER.
Great Mullisheg is royal.

GOODLACK.
False to you.

BESS.
Gracious and kind.

ROUGHMAN.
Disloyal to us all.

SPENCER.
Wrap me not in these wonders, worthy friend.

GOODLACK.
The King still loves your Bess.

SPENCER.
Hah!

ROUGHMAN.
The Queen your Spencer.

BESS.
How!

GOODLACK.
This night he must enjoy her.

ROUGHMAN.
And she him.

SPENCER.
I'll make my passage through the blood of Kings,
Rather than suffer this.

BESS.
I through hell.

GOODLACK.
Else all die.

CLEM.
Die? 'Sfoot! This is worse than being made an eunuch.

BESS.
Why, Captain, why, Lieutenant, had you the skill
To bring my ship thus far, to wreck her here?
Thou, Tom Goodlack, canst thou fail me now?

GOODLACK.
I study for you.

SPENCER.
Have you way?

GOODLACK.
'Tis but a desperate course; but if it fail –

SPENCER.
If thou hast any project –

BESS.
Joy or comfort –

ROUGHMAN.
And if not comfort, counsel –

GOODLACK.
Say it thrive?

BESS.
What, Captain? What?

SPENCER.
No longer hold us in suspense, good Captain.

GOODLACK.
You, noble friend,
This night cast gracious eyes upon the Queen.

BESS.
And prove to me disloyal?

GOODLACK.
You, fair Bess,
With amorous favours entertain the King.

SPENCER.
And yield herself to his intemperate lust?

ROUGHMAN.
Hear him out.

GOODLACK.
You soothe the Queen, I'll flatter with the King.
Let's promise fair on both sides –

SPENCER.
The event of this?

GOODLACK.
A happy freedom, with a safe escape
Unto our ship this night. Where's Clem?

CLEM.
Noble Captain.

GOODLACK.

Post to the ship; bid Fawcett man the long boat
With ten good musketeers and, at a watchword,
If we can free our passage, take us in.
Nay, make haste; one minute's stay is death.

CLEM.

I am gone in a twinkling.

GOODLACK.

To compass the King's signet; then to command
Our passage, 'scape the gates and watches too:
Hours waste, revels come on.
Let no distaste nor discontented brow
Appear in you. Disperse; the King's on coming.

Enter Mullisheg, Tota, Joffer and Alcade.

MULLISHEG.

We consecrate this evening, beauteous bride,
To th'honour of your nuptials. – Is all done?

GOODLACK.

Done.

TOTA.

Is he ours?

ROUGHMAN.

Yours.

TOTA.

And we ever thine.

GOODLACK.

Your Highness's signet, to command our passage
From chamber to chamber.

MULLISHEG.

'Tis there.

GOODLACK.

The word.

MULLISHEG.

'Tis Mullisheg.

We keep the bride
Too long from rest; now she is free for bed.

TOTA.

Please her to accept it,
In honour of her beauty; this night I'll do her any service.

BESS.

Mighty princess,
The fashion of our country is not to trust

The secrets of a nuptial night like this
To the eyes of any stranger.

TOTA.

At your pleasure.

Remember.

ROUGHMAN.

'Tis writ here.

MULLISHEG.

Captain.

Exeunt. Manet Goodlack.

GOODLACK.

I am fast, – Auspicious Fate, thy aid,
To guard the honour of this English maid.

Exit.

Enter Roughman, ushering the Queen.

ROUGHMAN.

Tread soft, good madam.

TOTA.

Is this the chamber?

ROUGHMAN.

I'll bring him instantly.
He thinks this bed provided for his Bess.
Beware; be not too loud, lest that your tongue betray you.

TOTA.

Mute as night;
Haste time, and haste our bounty.

ROUGHMAN.

Queen, I shall.

Exit.

Enter Goodlack and Mullisheg.

GOODLACK.

My Lord, the custom is in England still
For maids to go to bed before their husbands:

MULLISHEG.

And in the dark?

GOODLACK.

We use it for the most part.
This is the place where Bess expects her Spencer.

MULLISHEG.

Thou Viceroy of Argiers –

GOODLACK.
Not too loud.
Why enters not Your Highness? You are safe.

MULLISHEG.
With as much joy as to our prophet's rest.
But what thinks Spencer of this?

GOODLACK.
I have shifted in her place
A certain Moor, whom I have hired for money,
Which (poor soul) he entertains for Bess.

MULLISHEG.
My excellent friend.

GOODLACK.
Beware of conference, lest your tongue reveals
What this safe darkness hides.

MULLISHEG.
I am all silent. –
Oh! thou contentful night, into thy arms,
Of all that e'er I tasted, sweetest and best,
I throw me, more for pleasure than for rest.

Exit Mullisheg.

Enter Bess, Spencer and Roughman.

SPENCER.
How goes the night?

ROUGHMAN.
'Tis some two hours from day.

BESS.
Yet no news from the Captain.

ROUGHMAN.
I have done a midwife's part: I have brought the Queen to bed;
I could do no more.

Enter Goodlack.

SPENCER.
The Captain is come.

BESS.
Thy news?

GOODLACK.
All safe. I have left them at it.

BESS.
King and Queen?

GOODLACK.
The same.

ROUGHMAN.
Now for us.
I have here the King's signet; this will yield us
Way through the court and city: Bess being mask'd
How can she be described, when none suspect?
Ay, there's all the danger.

GOODLACK.
                         There's one bashaw,
Whose eye is fix'd on Spencer, and he now
Walks e'en before our lodging. He and I
May freely pass the court; and you, fair Bess,
I would disguise: but then for Spencer?

BESS.
Why, that's the main of all: all, without his freedom,
That we can aim at's nothing.

SPENCER.
With this signet you three shall pass to th' ship:
Whilst I'm in sight, she will not be suspected.
My escape leave to my own fair fortune.

BESS.
How that?

SPENCER.
Through twenty bashaws I will hew my way.
But I will see thee ere morning.

BESS.
It is our wedding night;
Wouldst now divide us?

GOODLACK.
Words are vain.
We now must cleave to action.

SPENCER.
Bess, be sway'd.

BESS.
To go to sea without thee,
And leave thee subject unto a tyrant's cruelty?
I'll die a thousand deaths first.

SPENCER.
First save one,
And by degrees the rest.

GOODLACK.
Talk yourselves
To your deaths, do: will you venture forth?
Leave me to the bashaw.

ROUGHMAN.
Or me.

SPENCER.
Neither.
Conduct her safe: th' advantage of the night
I'll take for my escape; and, my sweet Bess,
If in the morning I behold thee not
Be assur'd I am dead.

BESS.
And if thou diest tomorrow, be assur'd
Tomorrow I'll be with thee.

SPENCER.
Shall thy love
Betray us all to death?

BESS.
Well, I will go.

SPENCER.
Of the Moor's bounty bear not anything
Unto our ship, lest they report of us
We fled by night, and robb'd them.

GOODLACK.
Nobly resolv'd.

SPENCER.
Farewell, Bess.

GOODLACK.
Will you mask yourself?
Ho! Porter!

Enter Porter.

PORTER.
Who calls?

GOODLACK.
One from the King.

PORTER.
How shall I know that?

GOODLACK.
This token be your warrent: behold his signet.

PORTER.
That's not enough: the word?

GOODLACK.
Mullisheg.

PORTER.
Some weighty business is in hand,
That the King's signet is abroad so late.
Pass freely. –

Enter Bashaw Alcade.

ALCADE.
On his marriage night, and up at this hour! I much suspect,
these English 'mongst themselves are treacherous. The King
had conference with the Captain: and now the King hath
removed his lodging, and it may be to prostitute the English
maid. Hah! Suspect, said I? It must needs be so: troth, I could
even pity this poor forlorn Englishman, who this night must be
forced to lie alone, and have the King taste for him.
What! Up so late, and on your bridal night,
When you should lie lull'd in the fast embrace
Of your fair mistress. –

SPENCER.
Sure, this Moor hath been made private to the King's intents.
Is't possible,
To lodge my bride in one place, and dispose me
To a wrong chamber? She not once send to me,
That I might know to find her.

ALCADE.
Excellent!

SPENCER.
I'll not take't
At the hands of an empress, much less at hers.

ALCADE.
Oh! I guess the cause of your grief.

SPENCER.
And, sir, you may; but I'll be revenged.

ALCADE.
Troth, and I would.

SPENCER.
I'll bosom somebody,
Be it the common'st courtezan in Fez.

ALCADE.
Can you do less?

SPENCER.
To leave me the first night.

ALCADE.
Oh! 'Twas a sign she never lov'd you.

SPENCER.
I perceive, Bashaw Alcade, you understand my wrongs.

ALCADE.
In part.

SPENCER.
Your word is warrant: pass me the court gate.
I'll to some loose bordello, and tell her when I have done.
Make me wait thus!

ALCADE.
Oh! sir, 'tis insufferable.

SPENCER.
Troth, I dally my revenge too long.

ALCADE.
What ho!

Enter Porter.

PORTER.
How now! Who calls?

ALCADE.
Bashaw Alcade: turn the key.

PORTER.
Pass freely.

SPENCER.
Sir, I am bound to you.
To take this wrong, I should be held no man.

Exit Spencer.

ALCADE.
Ha, ha! Porter, now he's without, let him command his
entrance no more, neither for reward nor entreaty, till day
breaks.

PORTER.
Sir, he shall not.

ALCADE.
Mullisheg will give me great thanks for this.
I'll to his chamber, there attend without,
Till he shall waken.

Scene Nineteen

The bridge.
Alarum.
Enter Joffer, Lieutenant; Spencer prisoner and wounded.

JOFFER.
When I behold the slaughter you have made,
I wish you had escap'd, not been made captive
To him, who though he may admire and love you,
Yet cannot help you.

SPENCER.
Your style is like your birth, Joffer.
Speak: what's my danger?

JOFFER.
Know, sir, a double forfeit of your life.

SPENCER.
I was born to't, and I embrace my fortune.

JOFFER.
We know your name, and now have prov'd your courage:
You are free from irons.

SPENCER.
When this news shall come to her!

JOFFER.
Lieutenant, lead the watch some distance off;
Leave him to my charge – In you – I have observ'd
Strange contrarieties, I much muse
Why either such a small effuse of blood,
Or the pale fear of death,
Should have the power to force a tear from such
A noble eye.

SPENCER.
I tell thee, Bashaw Joffer,
The rack, strappado or the scalding oil,
The burning pincers or the boiling lead,
The stakes, the pikes, the cauldron or the wheel,
Were all these tortures to be felt an once,
Could not draw water hence.

JOFFER.
Whence comes it, then?

SPENCER.
Oh! Bess, Bess, Bess, Bess.
If you have ever lov'd, or such a maid,
So fair, so constant, and so chaste as mine,
How would it melt in you!

JOFFER.
Sir, you confound me.

SPENCER.
I will be brief. The travels of my Bess,

To find me out, you have partook at full,
Now, when we come to sum up all our joy,
And this night were ent'ring to our hoped bliss,
The King – oh, most unworthy of that name! –
He quite fell off from goodness.

JOFFER.

                              Who – Mullisheg?

SPENCER.

His lust outweigh'd his honour; he laid plots
To take this sweet night from me; but prevented,
I have convey'd my beauteous bride aboard,
My Captain and Lieutenant.

JOFFER.

                              Are they escap'd?

SPENCER.

Safe to our merchant's ship. Thus fortune let me
Through many dangers, till I pass'd this bridge,
The last of all your watches. When we parted, I swore,
If I surviv'd, to visit her aboard
By such an hour; but if I fail, that she
Should think me dead: now, if I break one minute,
She leaps into the sea. 'Tis this, great Bashaw,
That from a soldier's eyes draws tears.

JOFFER.

You have deeply touch'd me; and to let you know
All moral virtues are not solely grounded
In th' hearts of Christians, go, and pass free;
I will conduct you past all danger; but, withal,
Remember my head's left to answer it.

SPENCER.

Now I may say, in Barbary I found
A rare black swan?

JOFFER.

                        Your anchors,
They are soon weigh'd, and you have sea-room free
To pass unto your country. 'Tis but my life;
And I shall think it nobly spent to save you.

SPENCER.

Appoint me a fix'd hour: if I return not,
May I be held a recreant to my country.

JOFFER.

By noon tomorrow.

SPENCER.

                              Bind me by some oath.

JOFFER.

Only your hand and word.

SPENCER.

                        Which if I break –

JOFFER.

I'll bear you past all watches.

                                        Exeunt.

Scene Twenty

The palace.
    Enter Mullisheg and Tota.

MULLISHEG.

The morning calls me from the sweet embraces
Of the fair English damsel.

TOTA.

                        The English stranger
Is stol'n from forth mine arms; I am at full reveng'd.
Were I again to match, I'd marry one
Of this brave nation,
They are such sweet and loving bedfellows,
Now to my chamber: darkness guide my way.

MULLISHEG.

Venetian ladies, nor the Persian girls,
The French, the Spanish, nor the Turkish dames,
Ethiop, nor Greece, kiss with half the art
These English can.

Enter Bashaw Alcade.

Oh! I have had the sweetest night's content
That ever King enjoy'd.

ALCADE.

                        With the fair English bride.

MULLISHEG.

Nor envy if I raise the Captain for't,
For he shall mount.

ALCADE.

I had a hand in't, too, I spied the bridegroom,
As still mine eyes were fix'd on him, up and late;

Then, by a trick, a pretty sleight, a fine fetch of mine own,
I pass'd him forth the gates, and gave command
He should not have his entrance back again.

MULLISHEG.
Your aim in that?

ALCADE.
For fear lest he by some suspicious jealousy
Should have disturb'd your rest.

MULLISHEG.
This makes thee of our Council.

ALCADE.
                  'Tis an honour
My wisdom hath long aim'd at.

Enter a Guard.

GUARD.
Pardon, great King, that I thus rudely press
Into your private bed-chamber.

MULLISHEG.
               Speak; thy news?

GUARD.
With your Highness' signet and the word,
The English captain, with the lovely bride,
And her lieutenant, hath secretly this night,
Pass'd the court gates, pass'd all the watches, and
Got aboard their vessel.
And I was sent to know Your Highness' pleasure.

MULLISHEG.
Hah! This night? – Alcade, seek, search;
I left her sleeping in our royal bed.

ALCADE.
I shall, my lord. – I half suspect.

                           Exit.

MULLISHEG.
But was not Spencer with them?

GUARD.
Only they three.

Re-enter Bashaw Alcade.

MULLISHEG.
We are amaz'd.
Alcade, whom find'st thou there?

ALCADE.
Nothing, my lord, but empty sheets,
A bed new toss'd, but neither English lady,
Nor any lady else.

MULLISHEG.
We stand astonish'd,
Not knowing what to answer.

Enter a second messenger.

MESSENGER.
Pardon, great King, if I relate the news
That will offend you highly.

MULLISHEG.
The English captain, lady, and lieutenant are escap'd?

MESSENGER.
But that's not all. Spencer, without
The signet or the word, being left behind.

MULLISHEG.
(*to Alcade*). You call'd the porter up,
And let him after.

ALCADE.
Pardon, great King.

MULLISHEG.
Was this your trick, your sleight, your strategem?
As we are King of Fez, thy life shall pay.

MESSENGER.
Then pass'd he to the bridge,
Where stood armed men, in number forty.
Six, to the maze
Of all the rest, were slain: nor would he yield,
At which the captain of the watch came down,
And there surpris'd him.

MULLISHEG.
Is he prisoner, then?

MESSENGER.
In custody of the great Bashaw Joffer,
With whom we left him.

MULLISHEG.
Command our bashaw
To bring him clogg'd in irons. – These English pirates
Have robb'd us of much treasure; and for that
His trait'rous life shall answer.

ALCADE.
What I did was merely ignorance.

MULLISHEG.
Nay, bribes;
And I shall find it so. – Bear him to guard. –

Exit Alcade, guarded.

What dissolute strumpet did that trait'rous captain
Send to our sheets?

Scene Twenty-one

The ship.
Enter Captain Goodlack, Bess, Roughman, Clem.

BESS.
I prithee, Roughman, step into my cabin,
And bring me here my hour-glass.

ROUGHMAN.
That I shall.

GOODLACK.
To what end would you use it?

BESS.
I would know how long I have to live.

Enter Roughman with the glass.

ROUGHMAN.
Your glass.

BESS.
Gramercy, good Lieutenant.
No news from Fawcett yet, that waits for Spencer.
The long boat's not returned?

GOODLACK.
Not yet.

BESS.
Clem, to the main-top, Clem. The day is broke already.

CLEM.
With all my heart, so you will give me warning before the
gunner shoots, lest I tumble down again.

BESS.
Prithee, begone: let's have no jesting now.

GOODLACK.
How fares it with you, Bess?

BESS.
What! No news yet?

GOODLACK.
None.

BESS.
Have you been all at prayers?

BOTH.
We have.

BESS.
I thank you, gentlemen. Never more need:
Dost thou not think, Captain, my Spencer's slain?

GOODLACK.
Yet hope the best.

BESS.
This is the hour he promis'd: Captain, look,
For I have not the heart, and truly tell me
How far 'tis spent.

GOODLACK.
Some fifteen minutes.

BESS.
Alas! No more? I prithee, tak't away;
Even just so many have I left to pray.

CLEM.
News, news, news!

BESS.
Good or bad?

CLEM.
Excellent, most excellent; nay, super-excellent. Fawcett and all
his companions are rowing hither like madmen; and there is
one that sits i' th' stern, and does not row at all; and that is – let
me see who is it? I am sure 'tis he – noble Spencer.

BESS.
Spencer! – Art thou sure?

CLEM.
I think you'll make a man swear his heart out.

BESS.
How shall I bear me, Captain, that my joy
Do not transcend my soul out of this earth,
Into the air, with passionate ecstasy?

Enter Spencer.

GOODLACK.
Now, farewell Barbary. King Mullisheg,
We have sea-room and wind at will: not ten
Of thy best galleys, arm'd with Moors,
Can fetch us back.

ROUGHMAN.
                    For England, gentlemen!

BESS.
Oh! where's the gunner?
See all the ordnance be straight discharg'd,
For joy my Spencer lives.

ROUGHMAN.
To make the Queen vex and torment herself.

BESS.
To make the King tear his contorted locks,
Dance, my soul,
And caper in my bosom, joyful heart,
That I have here my Spencer.

GOODLACK.
                    Come, weigh anchor.

SPENCER.
Captain, stay.

BESS.
Good, what's the cause? Canst though conceal't from me?
What! From thy Bess? Whence came that sigh?
You will not tell me. No; do not:
Come, I will know the cause.

SPENCER.
                    Know all in one:
Now I have seen you, I must leave you, Bess.

BESS.
Leave me?

She swoons.

SPENCER.
It must be spoke again, for I must leave you.
My honour, faith, and country, are engaged.

GOODLACK.
Sir, resolve us:
You wrap us in a labyrinth of doubts.

SPENCER.
I made my way through slaughter; but at length
The watch came down, and took me prisoner
Unto a noble bashaw
That, on my word and promise to return
By such an hour, he left himself in hostage.

GOODLACK.
But what's the lives of twenty thousand Moors,
To one that is a Christian?

ROUGHMAN.
Shall we give ourselves up to voluntary bondage.

BESS.
Prize you my love no better, than to rate it
Beneath the friendship of a barbarous Moor?

SPENCER.
I prize my honour, and a Christian's faith.
Above what earth can yield.

BESS.
Oh, my fate! Was ever maid thus cross'd,
That have so oft been brought to see my bliss,
And never taste it?
To meet my Spencer living, after death,
To join with him in marriage, not enjoy him?
To have him here, free from the barbarous Moors,
And now to lose him? Being so oft rais'd
To make my ruin greater. Then, false man, know
That thou hast taught me harshness. I without
Thee came to Mamorah, and to my country back
I will return without thee.
E'en at thy pleasure be it; my way's into my country.
Farewell; I'll not shed one tear more.

SPENCER.
And if I fail one minute, he must die.
The long boat now! – Farewell, Bess.
Ah Bess, I always lov'd thee.

                                        Exit Spencer.

BESS.
Why, farewell.

Scene Twenty-two

The palace.
Enter Mullisheg, Queen, Joffer, Headsman.

MULLISHEG.
Produce your prisoner, Bashaw.
We have vow'd his death, and he shall therefore die.
Go, bring him forth.

JOFFER.
Spare me, my lord, but some few hours, I shall.

MULLISHEG.
The least delay is death.

JOFFER.
Then know, my lord, he was my prisoner.

MULLISHEG.
How! Was, and is not?

JOFFER.
By promise –

MULLISHEG.
Not in gyves?

JOFFER.
He's gyved to me by faith, but else at liberty.

MULLISHEG.
Where is the English prisoner?

JOFFER.
I gave him freedom to his ship,
Upon his promise to return, by noon.
Now, if there be such nobleness in a Christian,
Which, being a Moor, I have express'd to him,
He will not see me perish.

MULLISHEG.
                    Foolish Bashaw,
To jest away thy head. You are all conspirators
Against our person, and you all shall die.
Why, canst thou think a stranger, so remote
Both in country and religion, being embark'd
At sea, and under sail, will expose himself
To voluntary dangers, for a bare verbal promise
And return?

The bell strikes noon.

The hour is past; the Christian hath broke faith. –
Off with his head!

Enter Spencer.

SPENCER.
                    Yet come at last.

MULLISHEG.
Is't possible? Can England, so far distant,
Harbour such noble virtues?

JOFFER.
I wish this blood, which now are friendly tears.
You are come unto your death.

SPENCER.
Great Mullisheg, cherish this noble Moor,
Whom all thy confines cannot parallel.

MULLISHEG.
Thou hast slain six of our subjects.

JOFFER.
                    Oh! Had you seen
But with what eminent valour –

MULLISHEG.
                    Naught that's ill
Can be well done: then, Bashaw, speak no more.
His life is merely forfeit; and he shall pay it.

SPENCER.
I am proud, Fez, that I now owe thee nothing.

MULLISHEG.
Englishman,
There's but one way for thee to save thy life
From imminent death.

SPENCER.
                    Well, propose it.

MULLISHEG.
                    Instantly
Send to thy vessel – and surrender up
Thy captain and thy fair bride: otherwise,
Thou shalt not live an hour.

SPENCER.
I pity and despise thy tyranny:
Not live an hour? And when my head is off,
What canst thou do then? But for her,
Wert thou the king of all the kings on earth;
Emperor of the universal empery,
Rather than yield my basest ship-boy up,
To become thy slave, much less betray my bride
To thee and to thy brutish lust, know, King

Of Fez, I'd die a hundred thousand deaths first.

MULLISHEG.
I'll try your patience. – Off with his head!

Enter Bess, Goodlack and Roughman.

BESS.
                              Stay!
If you love blood, I bring thee three for one.
What says't thou to it?

SPENCER.
I could be angry with you above measure.

MULLISHEG.
Captain, art thou there? Howe'er these fare,
Thou shalt be sure to pay for't.

GOODLACK.
                    'Tis least my care.

TOTA.
What groom betray'd you to our sheets?

ROUGHMAN.
'Twas the King: conceal what's past.

TOTA.
Howe'er my mind, then yet my body's chaste.

ROUGHMAN.
Make use on't.

SPENCER.
Dismiss, great King, these to their ship again.

BESS.
It were no justice, King, to forfeit his life,
And to spare mine.

GOODLACK.
I led them on, and therefore first should die.

ROUGHMAN.
I am as deep as any.

BESS.
Why pause you, King?

MULLISHEG.
Shall lust in me have chief predominance,
And virtuous deeds be quite exil'd?
Shall Christians have the honour
To be sole heirs of goodness, and we Moors
Barbarous and bloody? – Captain, resolve me,

What common courtezan didst thou convey
Into our royal bed?

TOTA.
              Pardon me, great King;
I, having private notice of your plots,
Wrought him unto my purpose; and 'twas I
Lodg'd in your arms that night.

MULLISHEG.
– English maid,
We give thee once more back unto thy husband,
Whom likewise freely we receive to grace;
And, as amends for our pretended wrongs,
With her we'll tender such an ample dower,
As shall renown our bounty. But we fear
We cannot recompence the injurious loss
Of your last night's expectations.
Captain, we prize thy virtues to thy friends,
And, Bashaw, for thy nobleness to a gentleman
We here create thee Viceroy of Argiers,
Y'have quench'd in me all lust, by which shall grow
Virtues which Fez and all the world shall know.

BESS.
And now, my Spencer, after all our troubles,
Crosses, and threat'nings of the sea's rough brow,
I ne'er could say that thou wert mine own till now.

MULLISHEG.
A golden Girl th'art call'd; and, wench, be bold,
Thy lading back shall be with pearl and gold.

Exeunt.